How precious is your steadfast love, O God!
   The children of mankind take refuge in the shadow of your wings.
They feast on the abundance of your house,
   and you give them drink from the river of your delights.

                                                (Psalm 36:7-8)

RIVER OF DELIGHTS

QUENCHING YOUR THIRST FOR JOY
VOLUME 1

RICK HOWE

BOOKS BY RICK HOWE

Path of Life: Finding the Joy You've Always Longed For, 2012, University Ministries Press Revised Edition, 2017. 279 pages.

River of Delights: Quenching Your Thirst For Joy, Volume 1, 2015, University Ministries Press Revised Edition, 2017. 230 pages.

River of Delights: Quenching Your Thirst For Joy, Volume 2, 2015, University Ministries Press Revised Edition, 2017. 250 pages.

Living Waters: Daily Refreshment for Joyful Living, 2017, University Ministries Press. 393 pages.

Reasons of the Heart: Joy and the Rationality of Faith, 2017, University Ministries Press. 250 pages.

FOR SMALL GROUP STUDIES

Enjoying God: Discovering the Greatest of All Pleasures, University Ministries Press, 2017. 122 pages.

Love's Delights: The Joys of Marriage and Family, University Ministries Press, 2017. 104 pages.

Sacred Patterns: Work, Rest, and Play in a Joyful Vision of Life, University Ministries Press, 2017. 122 pages.

Kingdom Manifesto: A Call to Joyful Activism, University Ministries Press, 2017. 104 pages.

Joy and the Problem of Evil, University Ministries Press, Boulder, 2017. 122 pages.

For more information, visit www.rickhowe.org.

University Ministries Press

Boulder, Colorado

Copyright © 2015 Rick Howe

University Ministries Press Revised Edition, 2017.

Scripture quotations are from The Holy Bible, English Standard Version® (ESV®), copyright © 2001 by Crossway, a publishing ministry of Good News Publishers. Used by permission. All rights reserved.

Scripture taken from the Holy Bible, NEW INTERNATIONAL VERSION®. Copyright © 1973, 1978, 1984 by Biblica, Inc. All rights reserved worldwide. Used by permission. NEW INTERNATIONAL VERSION® and NIV® are registered trademarks of Biblica, Inc. Use of either trademark for the offering of goods or services requires the prior written consent of Biblica US, Inc.

Revised Standard Version of the Bible, copyright ©1952 [2nd edition, 1971] by the Division of Christian Education of the National Council of the Churches of Christ in the United States of America. Used by permission. All rights reserved.

New Revised Standard Version Bible, copyright © 1989 Division of Christian Education of the National Council of the Churches of Christ in the United States of America. Used by permission. All rights reserved.

Any people depicted in stock imagery provided by iStockPhoto are models, and such images are being used for illustrative purposes only. Certain stock imagery © iStockPhoto.

ISBN: 978-0-9987859-3-6

To Amberle, Lorien, and Jamison
My Joy and Crown

ABBREVIATIONS

JB	The Jerusalem Bible
JBP	The New Testament in Modern English, by J.B. Phillips
KJV	King James Version
NASB	New American Standard Bible
NIV	New International Version of the Bible
NRSV	New Revised Standard Version Bible
RSV	Revised Standard Version of the Bible

CONTENTS

Author's Note 1

Preface 2

1 Enjoying God 4

2 Joy and the Glory of God 16

3 Enjoying God's World 30

4 The Joy of Salvation 47

5 Joy and the Word of God 61

6 Encountering God in His Word 74

7 Joy and Circumstances: Misunderstandings 83

8 Finding Joy in the Circumstances of Life 92

9 Marriage: Eden's Joy 105

10 Marriage: Far as the Curse is Found 115

11 Marriage and Family: Eden and More 125

12 Marriage and Family: Love's Delights, Part 1 136

13 Marriage and Family: Love's Delights, Part 2 145

About the Author 157

Endnotes 158

AUTHOR'S NOTE

I didn't set out to write books about joy. Joy beckoned, I followed, and the quest has found literary expression in *Path of Life: Finding the Joy You've Always Longed For*, *River of Delights: Quenching Your Thirst for Joy*, *Living Water: Daily Refreshment for Joyful Living*, and *Reasons of the Heart: Joy and the Rationality of Faith*.

The apostle Paul wrote to the church in Rome: "The gifts and the calling of God are irrevocable." I've done many other things over the years, but my work on joy has seemed very much like a gift and a calling. I've been wonderfully enriched by it, and at the same time have felt summoned to pursue it. I believe that God is behind both. My prayer is that this gift and this calling will bear fruit for his Kingdom.

As you will see, there are many endnotes in *River of Delights*, including Scripture references, references to other works, as well as my own comments. My suggestion is that you read *River of Delights* first without interacting with the endnotes in order to trace the flow of thought without interruption, and then read it again with those references for a more robust learning experience.

The "Questions for Thought and Discussion" for each chapter reflect my hope that you will study this book with others, my belief that learning in community is the best way to learn, and my prayer that God will use this book to create communities of joy for the advancement of his Kingdom.

PREFACE

An apocalyptic foreboding has many in its grip, strengthened by endless newsfeeds and broadcasts featuring economic woes, violence, terrorism, wars and threats of war, corruption in high places, depletion of energy resources, global climate change, natural catastrophes, pestilence, and toxins in our environment and our food.

No wonder words like *anxiety, depression, melancholy, and stress* are used to describe our generation! Historians in the future might well call ours *The Age of Prozac*. Depressive disorders are widespread. The pharmaceutical industry has grown rich on them.

The fact that this emotional epidemic grows unabated should signal the possibility that we have misdiagnosed and mistreated the problem. I don't deny that there are frightening factors behind our personal angst and cultural malaise, but I believe that there is an underlying cause that we ignore at our own greater peril. We are disoriented and dysfunctional. We are disoriented because we have removed God from our vision of life, and dysfunctional because we attempt vainly to live without him. Much else (economic woes, violence, toxins in our environment, *et al*) results directly or indirectly from this.

"A joyful heart is a good medicine."[1] This was once proverbial wisdom. It is true because joy connects us with God, and that is the healthiest place for us to be. Dallas Willard wrote, "Full joy is our first line of defense against weakness, failure, and disease of mind and body."[2] Peter Kreeft says much the same: "A joyful spirit inspires joyful feelings and even a more psychosomatically healthy body. (For example, we need less sleep when we have joy and have more resistance to all kinds of diseases from colds to cancers.)"[3] This ancient wisdom deserves a revival in our day. In fact, it is our only hope.

The premises of this book are that joy links us with God, it can touch and transform every dimension of our lives, and we will flourish only as we position ourselves to receive this gift from Him.

Let's listen in on the worship of the Psalmist:

> Your steadfast love, O LORD, extends to the heavens,
>   your faithfulness to the clouds.
> Your righteousness is like the mountains of God;
>   your judgments are like the great deep;
>   man and beast you save, O LORD.
> How precious is your steadfast love, O God!
>   The children of mankind take refuge in the shadow of your wings.
> They feast on the abundance of your house,
>   and you give them drink from the river of your delights.
> For with you is the fountain of life;
>   in your light do we see light. (Psalm 36:5-9)

If you are open to the Voice that beckons in these words, welcome to *River of Delights*!

CHAPTER 1

ENJOYING GOD

Imagine a room with high-backed chairs around a great oaken table, set with plates, silverware, goblets, and bowls. There are pitchers filled with fruity refreshment, and baskets with rolls hot from an oven. The aroma fills your senses and draws you in. You can almost taste the pastry and melting butter. On the other side of a door, partly closed, you hear bustling, merry singing, and the clanking of pots and pans. The wondrous smells of unseen cuisine waft into the room. You can't remember the last time you ate. It must have been ages ago!

You've been invited to a banquet. Take your place at the table and prepare for something exquisite. We will feast from the bounty of God's house. Our drink has been fetched from the river of his delights:

> How precious is your steadfast love, O God!
>   The children of mankind take refuge in the shadow of your wings.
> They feast on the abundance of your house,
>   and you give them drink from the river of your delights.
>   (Psalm 36:7-8)

Here is the first and most important thing for you to know in order to fill your hungry, thirsty heart: Joy is the greatest of all pleasures, and the enjoyment of God is the greatest of all joys.[1] Joy is the best gift we can possibly receive, because the Giver offers himself in his gift, and he is supreme.

The enjoyment of God is not only the greatest of all joys, it is the Joy in every joy. Wherever there is true joy, God is in it, whether he is beheld in the enraptured gaze of our hearts, or is the Light by which other pleasures are illumined and experienced as his good gifts.[2] Joy always has to do with God. Always. *Whether we know it or not, our experience of joy in every instance is a connection with God.*[3] If we are held in hushed delight before a forest ablaze with autumn color, we have encountered the Creator in his artistry. If we revel in a sumptuous meal and find ourselves savoring the experience with a thankful heart, we have tasted his goodness. If we find pleasure in people, it is an enjoyment of God mirrored in them,[4] and, among those who are being redeemed, the habitation of God within them.[5]

There is no joy apart from God. It is not even possible. To speak of joy without speaking of God is a desecration of language. If we knew the true nature and dimensions of joy, we would see that it is always, and never less than, our heart's encounter with the Joyful One. Joy is the touch of God. The fragrance of his presence. A glimpse of his beauty. An echo of his voice.[6]

To say that we were created for God, and that we were made for joy, is to say the same thing in different ways. In words now famous, Augustine wrote, "You have formed us for yourself, and our hearts are restless until they find rest in You."[7] We are vagabonds, wandering restively in pursuit of something that beckons and yet eludes us until we find our hearts' true home in God. Pascal saw our quest for joy ending here:

There once was in man a true happiness of which there now remain to him only the mark and empty trace, which he in vain tries to fill from all his surroundings, seeking from things absent the help he does not obtain in things present. . . . But these are all inadequate, because the infinite abyss can only be filled by an infinite and immutable object, that is to say, only by God himself.[8]

The greatest joy in this world (and the next) is our hearts' delight in God.[9] For those who know it, nothing enriches life more. Nothing pleases more fully. Nothing satisfies the longings of our hearts more profoundly than a joy that is at the same time adoration and awe, reverence and rapture, breathtaking wonder and soul-satisfying pleasure. It is a delight in the beauty, majesty, and splendor of God, and then a joy that so great and glorious a God is ours.[10] The enjoyment of God leaves us incredulous, marveling, *"Surely this is too good to be true!"* But it is supremely good and it is true. It is a pleasure-filled wonder (or wonderful pleasure) that there should be such a God, and even greater pleasure and greater wonder that he offers himself to us for our joy.

ENJOYING GOD FOR WHO HE IS

God's joy, first, is his delight in himself.[11] He enjoys being God. He exults in his excellence. He rejoices in his regal splendor. He takes boundless pleasure in his infinite perfection. It is a good thing for us that he does! There would be no joy anywhere in the universe if he did not. God's joy is the fountain from which our joy flows. Ours is a share in his. Like his, our joy is first a delight in who God is. Not what he does *for* us, but who he is *to* us.[12] Jonathan Edwards wrote of this joy:

True saints have their minds, in the first place, inexpressibly pleased and delighted with the sweet ideas of the glorious and amiable nature of the things of God. And this is the spring of all their delights, and the cream of all their pleasures; 'tis the joy of their joy. This sweet and ravishing entertainment, they have in viewing the beautiful and delightful nature of divine things, is the foundation of the joy they have afterward in the consideration of their being theirs.[13]

We tend to approach the attributes of God abstractly.[14]   Apart from an encounter with God, our systematic theologies make his traits lifeless things to our hearts. Though it is scandalous to do so, we read about the holiness of God with a yawn. Isaiah encountered the Thrice Holy God and fell on his face as a dead man.[15] Though Heaven is appalled at the ingratitude, we take the goodness of God for granted. Barely able to contain himself, the Psalmist cried out, "O taste and see that the LORD is good!"[16] We treat his justice as the duty of deity. Sacred poets saw it inspiring the entire cosmos in a joyous song of praise:

Say among the nations, "The LORD reigns!
　Yea, the world is established, it shall never be moved;
　he will judge the peoples with equity."
Let the heavens be glad, and let the earth rejoice;
　let the sea roar, and all that fills it;
　let the field exult, and everything in it!
Then shall all the trees of the wood sing for joy
　before the LORD, for he comes,
　for he comes to judge the earth.
He will judge the world with righteousness,
　and the peoples with his truth. (Psalm 96:10-13)

To the astonishment of angels, we argue about divine sovereignty and human freedom. The very thought of a God who in sovereign generosity gives us liberty and in sovereign mercy forgives our sinful use of that gift led the apostle Paul not to debate but to worship:

> O the depth of the riches and the wisdom and knowledge of God!
> How unsearchable are his judgments and how inscrutable his ways!
>
> > "For who has known the mind of the Lord,
> > or who has been his counselor?"
> > "Or who has given a gift to him
> > that he might be repaid?"
>
> For from him and through him and to him are all things. To him
> be glory for ever. Amen. (Romans 11:33-36)[17]

The attributes of God are not textbook definitions. They are facets of who he is. Dimensions of deity that impinge upon us. Qualities of the One with whom we have to do.[18] We do not experience them in their fullness or crystalline clarity. In our present state we could bear neither. Nevertheless, in ways that are suited to our fallenness and finitude, God discloses himself to us, and in that circle of encounter we discover the joy for which we were made. Daily our hearts then echo the ancient prayer: "Satisfy us in the morning with your steadfast love (an experience of God, and not just a theological idea) so that we may rejoice and be glad all our days."[19]

ENJOYING GOD FOR WHAT HE DOES

God takes pleasure in all that he does and invites us to find our joy here, as well:

> Our God is in the heavens;
> he does all that he pleases. (Psalm 115:3)
>
> Whatever the LORD *pleases*, he does. (Psalm 135:6)

The LORD was pleased for his righteousness' sake, to magnify his law and make it glorious. (Isaiah 42:21)

I am the LORD who practices steadfast love, justice and righteousness in the earth; *for in these things I delight*, says the LORD. (Jeremiah 9:24)

I will make with them an everlasting covenant, that I will not turn away from doing good to them; and I will put the fear of me in their hearts, that they may not turn from me. *I will rejoice in doing them good . . . with all my heart and all my soul.* (Jeremiah 32:40-41)[20]

God is always active, which means that his joy in what he does is always full.[21] We have the barest glimpse of the smallest part of what he does in the world, but even this can bring joy. Imagine an awareness of his activity far greater than ours! Jesus saw God's presence and work in the world as no one else ever has:

Jesus said to them, "Truly, truly, I say to you, the Son can do nothing of his own accord, but only what he sees the Father doing. For whatever the Father does, that the Son does likewise. (John 5:19)

To his eyes this is a God-bathed, and God-permeated world. It is a world filled with a glorious reality, where every component is within the range of God's direct knowledge and control – though he obviously permits some of it, for good reasons, to be for a while otherwise than as he wishes. It is a world that is inconceivably beautiful and good because of God and because God is always in it. It is a world in which God is continually at play and over which he constantly rejoices.[22]

Joy is an interface between our hearts and God's activity in the world. It is a nexus between the two. The greater our knowledge of what God is doing, the greater our opportunities for joy; the greater our joy, the greater our incentive to discover what he is doing in the world.

Jesus invites us to share his vision of the world, and to enter into his joy, "that my joy may be in you and that your joy may be full," he said.[23] We don't need to have his knowledge of God's activity in the world; we need only to place our confidence in him, trust that his vision of the world is true, and ask him to show us more of what he sees.[24] Don't talk yourself out of this joy because it is beyond the boundaries of what you have experienced so far. And don't let others dissuade or discourage you because they are strangers to this. Jesus was not naïve! (If you believe that he was, I'm not sure how you can be his follower.) Your first step into his vision of the world and into his joy may be the prayer, "I believe. Help my unbelief!"[25] He takes pleasure in first steps. Even small steps. You will find joy with each one you take.

JOY IN THE TRIUNE GOD

The Trinity is not a doctrine dropped from the heavens in a theological treatise. It is a truth given in God's self-disclosure: a revelation whose original medium was the teaching of Jesus and the matching experience of his early followers.[26] (Without his teaching, his disciples would not have understood their experience; without their experience, his teaching would have been sounds in the air.)

The threefoldness of the one God was not a matter of theological calculus for our ancient brothers and sisters of faith, but a compelling dimension of their experience of God as he revealed himself to them. They came to know the one true God as Father, Son, and Holy Spirit.[27]

Joy in the Father. Jesus introduced his disciples to the fatherhood of God, and to the joys of knowing him this way. He taught them to address

God as *Abba* - the familiar and endearing term of a child for her father.[28] For those men and women the fatherhood of God was not a theological abstraction. It was an experience into which Jesus guided them. In the Father's power they found protection. In his providence they found direction. In his loving care they found supply for their needs. In his wisdom they found guidance for living well. In his Kingdom they found the greatest possible adventure, and the most significant investment of their lives.[29]

Joy in the Son. They discovered, however, that there was more to the fatherhood of God than their monotheistic minds were at first prepared to accept. The One who introduced them to God as their heavenly Father, and whose joy in the Father they shared, claimed deity for himself and called himself the Son.[30] He directed their joy not only to the Father, but to himself: "These things I have spoken to you, that my joy may be in you, and that your joy may be full."[31] Peter Kreeft sees the significance of this: "The man who said he was God also said he was our joy. If this claim is not true, it is the most blasphemous, egotistical, and insane thing ever spoken by human lips. If it is true, then God's single gift for all our desires is his Son. He *is* joy, joy alive and wearing a real human face. . . ." [32]

As unsettling as his claims must have been, his followers were compelled either to reject them or to accept them and make significant theological adjustments.[33] They were faced with the dilemma of dismissing Jesus or including him in their understanding of God. We know the cruciform reaction of their contemporaries. How would his disciples respond?

As they shared life with Jesus, they detected no flaw of sin.[34] As they watched and listened, they saw potency in his words and deeds that they had never witnessed before. When Jesus spoke, uncanny things happened. People were healed. Demons were cast out. The dead were raised to life. Storms were quelled. Multitudes were fed. And then there was his teaching! He stood the rabbinic world on its head, speaking as if he were the Authority above all human authorities.[35] His disciples were astonished as he assumed the divine prerogative of forgiving sin.[36] They were wide-eyed with wonder at his claims to have come from God and to be one with God.[37] They were startled by his declaration to be Lord of the Sabbath[38] and amazed at the unpretentious manner in which he saw himself as Lord of the Great Judgment awaiting all humanity at the end of days.[39] All of this was scandalous. Blasphemous! Or it was a window. A portal to a new but true understanding of God.[40]

As perplexing as these things must have been, his followers also found in Jesus the joy for which they longed, and which they had sought vainly in other things. In time they confessed what they did not fully comprehend, that the one God exists as Father and Incarnate Son.[41] In Jesus, the one God had come among them. To their enjoyment of the Father they were compelled to add a shared joy in the One who was uniquely the Father's Son.

Joy in the Spirit. Their joy and understanding of God became more richly colored and textured on the day of Pentecost when they were gifted and filled with the Holy Spirit.[42] They had been led by Jesus to expect a great event that would take place after his departure from them. He told them that the Spirit of Truth would come, sent by the Father to take his place upon the earth.[43] The Spirit would be distinct from the Son, and yet – in an utter mystery and a wondrous reality – would be the mode by which the risen Christ himself would be present among them.[44]

When that day came, another dimension was added to their joy. They had come to know joy in the Father and joy in the Son. From Pentecost on, they began to know joy in the Holy Spirit. In nuance it was different from the joy they had already learned, and yet it shared a kinship with their joy in the Father and their joy in Jesus. To some who looked on, this pleasure appeared to be the intoxication of wine.[45] To those who knew it in experience, however, it was the presence of the Spirit, welling up within them and overflowing in praise and an undaunted delight in proclaiming what God had done for them in Christ.

They experienced the Spirit as a Coming of Power.[46] A Clothing of Power.[47] They came to know him as Helper in the midst of life's challenges.[48] They discovered him as Teacher and Guide as they explored the new terrain of the Gospel.[49] They recognized him as Pledge and Guarantor, bearing witness with their spirits that they were children of God.[50] They knew him as Herald, inspiring deep within them the exultant cry, "Abba, Father!"[51] They found him to be the Source of their joy, even in the midst of hardship and persecution.[52]

We see a fledgling Trinitarian understanding of God in the benediction of Paul to the church in Corinth: "The grace of the Lord Jesus Christ and the love of God and the fellowship of the Holy Spirit be with you all."[53] This was meaningful to the Corinthian believers because it was true to their experience of God. They understood this way of speaking about God because they, too, had encountered him in these ways. As this joyful experience spread across the ancient world, and more and more came to speak this spiritually formed language, the doctrine of the Trinity emerged.[54]

Trinitarian joy. Augustine knew this joy in the Triune God: "The true objects of enjoyment, then, are the Father and the Son and the Holy Spirit, who are at the same time the Trinity, one Being, supreme above all, and common to all who enjoy Him."[55] I doubt that this three-faceted joy is as common today as Augustine believed it was in his fifth century world. To be generous to our generation, we are further removed from the epic events in the drama of redemption. Less generously (but more tellingly), we pay too little attention to what is already a slighter spiritual experience than our ancient brothers and sisters enjoyed. This is not a delight for debutants. Only serious (not to be mistaken for *somber*) followers of Jesus know it. It is a pleasure that flourishes in thoughtful hearts, in hearts that are habituated in worship of the Father, Son, and Spirit, in hearts that dance to songs of thanksgiving and praise to the Threefold God.

In this circle of encounter with God we discover the robust, three-dimensional joy that enriched the life of the early Church: joy in the Father for his work in creation and redemption, and for his provision and protective care; joy in the Son for his life among us, and for the blessings of salvation purchased through his death and resurrection; and joy in the Spirit who points us daily to Christ, and who dwells within us as an empowering presence and pledge of all that God has in store for us.[56]

QUESTIONS FOR THOUGHT AND DISCUSSION

1. If God has created a void within you that only he can fill, in what ways have you tried to fill that emptiness apart from God? With what things? What pursuits? What relationships? How do you see this playing out with your peers?

2. Why is it significant that our joy in God is linked to his joy in himself? Are there obstacles in your understanding of God that keep you from affirming his joy?

3. Why is it important to seek our joy first in who God is, and not what he can do for us? What are the implications of seeing God as a means to our ends, even if it is our own joy?

4. Describe experiences you have had in which you encountered God and became strikingly aware of some facet of his deity, e.g., his holiness, his goodness, his wisdom, his justice.

5. Can you identify nuances of joy in your relationship with God? Joy in the Father? Joy in the Son? Joy in the Spirit? If not, don't be discouraged! Let this be a catalyst for spiritual growth.

CHAPTER 2

JOY AND THE GLORY OF GOD

JOY AND GOD'S SELF-DISCLOSURE

God of glory,[1] King of glory,[2] Father of glory,[3] Majestic Glory.[4] Have you ever heard God addressed with these titles? Have you used them in prayer or in conversation with others? No? But they were given to us in the Scriptures, and they were given for a reason. Not only have they dropped out of our vocabulary of worship and prayer, they have all but vanished from our thoughts of God. We have lost ancient and important truths that were meant to shape our relationship with God, and we have been greatly impoverished as a result.

The glory of God, first, is all that he is in his transcendence over the world. It is his splendor, his magnificence, his majesty, and infinite worth. The glory of God is not a single attribute of God, but his nature in its fullness. In all that he is, God is glorious!

The fitting response of our hearts to the glory of God is reverence, wonder, and awe: a shudder at our own smallness, a shivering sense of the magnitude of God, a trembling delight in the grandeur of our God. Hearts that have been gripped by glory know the tremulous joy that so great a Being exists, and an astonishment-that-takes-one's-breath-away that so great a God invites us to know him and to enjoy him. It is a pleasure that is at once dread and delight, fear and fascination, amazement and adoration. To glorify God, first and foremost, is to acknowledge, confess, celebrate, and live our lives in light of God's glory. This is where joy is found. This is where our hearts discover pleasure in God.[5]

If this were all we knew about God's glory, it would fill our cup. But we must let it overflow, because this is only the truth by half. In the Sacred Word, *glory* not only describes God in himself, but God in his self-disclosure to us.[6] Let's explore this.

God is Spirit.[7] One thing about spirits is that they can't be discovered by our senses. They are invisible to us. In a hymn of praise, Paul wrote, "To the King of ages, immortal, *invisible*, the only God, be honor and glory for ever and ever. Amen."[8] Later in that same letter, he said that no one has ever seen God and no one can see him.[9] It is impossible because of who God is. The invisibility of God is fundamental Christian theology. If you want a visible and tangible deity you will have to find another religion, because Christianity insists that the true God can't be seen with our eyes or detected by our senses.

But that isn't all the Bible says about God. It also says that the invisible God reveals himself to people in visible and tangible ways. God's presence in the world is imperceptible, but the tokens of his presence are not. He dons a robe, as it were, to reveal himself to mortals.[10]   The Bible uses the word *glory* to describe his mantle. We can't see God, but we can behold his glory – the visible, tangible manifestation of the invisible, intangible God.[11] This is the second way in which the Bible uses the word *glory* in connection with God. Glory is what we encounter when God reveals himself in perceptible ways.

GOD'S GLORY IN NATURE

The heavens above us and the world around us brim with glory:

> The heavens are telling the glory of God. (Psalm 19:1)

> Holy, holy, holy is the LORD of hosts;
> The whole earth is full of his glory. (Isaiah 6:3)

Creation is filled with emblems of God's presence. The heavens are his crest, the earth his throne. His footmarks are everywhere, his fingerprints on all that he has made. If we see the world truly, it is not devoid of God (the mistake of Deism[12]), nor is it God (the error of Pantheism[13]), nor even the body of God (the false view of Panentheism[14]). It is a theater in which God displays his glory.[15]

We can make high stakes mistakes here. Those who venerate nature and bestow upon it the status of deity are in touch with the fact that there is more to the world than meets the eye. At some level they are aware that God is there. But they mistake his glory in the world for an identity with the world, and in doing so worship the creature rather than the Creator, who alone is worthy of praise.[16] If we acknowledge the creaturely status of the world, however, we are invited to enjoy the Creator in it, just as we enjoy a poet in her poem, an artist in his painting, or a composer in his music. Augustine put it this way:

> Let your mind roam through the whole creation; everywhere the created world will cry out to you: "God made me." Whatever pleases you in a work of art brings to your mind the artist who wrought it; much more, when you survey the universe, does the consideration of it evoke praise for its Maker. . . . Now if in considering these creatures of God human language is so at a loss,

what is it to do in regard to the Creator? When words fail, can aught but triumphant music remain?[17]

BEAUTY AND GLORY

The tangerine beauty of a sunset. The shimmering beauty of moonbeams on a lake. The distant beauty of a star-spangled sky. The brilliant beauty of sun-glistened snow. The lush beauty of a forest canopy. The arid beauty of a desert. The majestic beauty of mountains. The winged beauty of geese in flight. The underwater beauty of coral gardens. The thundering beauty of cascading waterfalls. The lustrous beauty of earthen gems. Beauty in the world is the glory of God.[18]

To learn from Augustine again:

> Question the beauty of the earth, question the beauty of the sea, question the beauty of the air, amply spread around everywhere, question the beauty of the sky, question the serried ranks of the stars, question the sun making the day glorious with is bright beams, question the moon tempering the darkness of the following night with its shining rays, question the animals that move in the waters, that amble about on dry land, that fly in the air . . . . They all answer you, 'Here we are, look; we're beautiful." Their beauty is their confession. Who made these beautiful changeable things, if not one who is beautiful and unchangeable?[19]

The beauty of creation is its confession. Our confession is taking pleasure in its beauty and responding to the Creator in adoration and awe.

I must warn you that there is both pleasure and peril in the beauty of the world: pleasure for those who enjoy it and whose hearts are filled with reverent appreciation, and peril for those who suppress the true significance of beauty and shut God out of their thoughts about the world. The apostle Paul wrote:

For the wrath of God is revealed from heaven against all ungodliness and unrighteousness of men, who by their unrighteousness suppress the truth. For what can be known about God is plain to them, because God has shown it to them. For his invisible attributes, namely, his eternal power and divine nature, have been clearly perceived, ever since the creation of the world, in the things that have been made. So they are without excuse. For although they knew God, they did not honor him as God or give thanks to him, but they became futile in their thinking, and their foolish hearts were darkened. (Romans 1:18-21)

We are surrounded on all sides by the glory of God in the beauty of his world. There is no escaping it! Our only choice is how we will respond to it. Beauty summons us to open our hearts to our Creator in pleasure and praise. In the beauty of the world God invites us to exalt him by exulting in all that he has made. If we refuse the invitation, beauty will rise in a gallery of witnesses to speak against us on the last day.

DIVINE VISITATIONS

Sometimes in the Scriptures God visits his people in dramatic ways. They see an aura of unearthly light. They become aware of a luminous presence. And they know that they have been visited by Heaven.[20] This, too, is God's glory:

When Moses came down from Mount Sinai, with the two tablets of the testimony in his hand as he came down from the mountain, Moses did not know that *the skin of his face shone because he had been talking with God.* Aaron and all the people of Israel saw Moses, and, behold, the skin of his face shone, and they were afraid to come near him. (Exodus 34:29-30)

(See Paul's commentary on this event: "The ministry of death, carved in letters on stone, came with such *glory* that the Israelites could not gaze at Moses' face because of its *glory*." 2 Corinthians 3:7, RSV)

Like the appearance of the bow that is in the cloud on the day of rain, so was the appearance of the *brightness all around*. Such was the appearance of the likeness of *the glory of the LORD*. And when I saw it, I fell on my face, and I heard the voice of one speaking. (Ezekiel 1:28)

And *the glory of the LORD* went up from the cherub to the threshold of the house, and the house was filled with the cloud, and the court was filled with *the brightness of the glory of the LORD*. (Ezekiel 10:4)

And in the same region there were shepherds out in the field, keeping watch over their flock by night. And an angel of the Lord appeared to them, and *the glory of the Lord shone around them, and they were filled with great fear.* (Luke 2:8-9)

God revealed his presence to his people in other ways, as well: through a burning bush,[21] pillars of cloud and fire,[22] in lightning and thunder,[23] and within the cloud-enshrouded tabernacle.[24] They were tokens of God's presence, emblems of his dwelling and activity among mortals.[25] They, too, are his glory.

What about Divine Visitations in our day? Does God still manifest his presence in auras of light, or in pillars of cloud and fire? Is it possible that we might come upon a bush that burns with the presence of God? It is within his power if it suits his purpose. The God who is present with us in every moment and in every place (whether we know it or not) can make his presence known in visible and tangible ways. It is important for us to affirm this. I have never witnessed a tornado moving ominously across the sky, but knowing that others have and can tell me about these sky funnels increases my respect for the power at work in our world. Even if we never have the experience ourselves, we should live in a state of openness to glory in the event that God surprises us! It is important for us to know that he is such a God. We should keep ourselves in a posture of readiness to encounter God in his incandescent presence and be amazed.

THE GRAIL OF GLORY

If God reveals his presence in the world, then the greatest adventure we can know is the quest to discover his glory. Our grail is not the famed cup of Christ, hidden to mortals, but God himself, disclosed to all who seek him:

> You will seek the LORD your God and you will find him, if you search after him with all your heart and with all your soul. (Deuteronomy 4:29)

> I love those who love me, and those who seek me diligently find me. (Proverbs 8:17)

> You will seek me and find me, when you seek me with all your heart. (Jeremiah 29:13)

> And without faith it is impossible to please him, for whoever would draw near to God must believe that he exists and that he rewards those who seek him. (Hebrews 11:6)

> May all who seek you
>   rejoice and be glad in you! (Psalm 40:16; 70:4)

Life at its best includes watching for God and his activity in our lives:

> O my Strength, I will watch for you,
>   for you, O God, are my fortress.
> My God in his steadfast love will meet me. (Psalm 59:8-9)

We ought to live each day with the hope and expectation of meeting God in whatever ways he may reveal his presence to us.[26] It is important for us to factor this into our understanding of God; otherwise we are in danger of a faith that becomes a mere abstraction and has little to do with our lives in the world. That may be the creed of Deists, who believe that God does not act in the world he made, but it is not the God and Father of our Lord Jesus Christ.[27]

Watch for things that don't fit the normal pattern of your experience. Look for the extraordinary in the course of the ordinary. For the unusual in the midst of the usual. For something that stands out to you as uncommon in what would otherwise be a common setting. A Presence. A Voice. A Shimmering. A Movement. A Perturbation. A subtle Change in the currents of the world around you.[28] Our quest to encounter God in his glory requires discernment and results in delight: discerning signs of God's presence in our lives, and delighting in them; looking for tangible tokens of the Intangible One wherever he bestows them, and rejoicing in that revelation. "May all who seek you rejoice and be glad in you!"[29]

God promises that those who seek him with whole hearts will find him. He is pleased with those who do. He rewards those who do.[30] The reward for seeking God? Finding him! This is where the glory is. This is where our joy will be.

GOODNESS AND GLORY

When Moses asked God, "Show me your glory" the response to him was, "I will make all my goodness pass before you, and will proclaim before you the name, The LORD. . . ."[31] Sometimes glory is a disclosure of the goodness of God, his moral excellence, or moral beauty.[32] To say that God is beautiful in this way is to say that he is to our hearts what a rainbow or a sunset is to our senses. What color, form, and texture are to a work of art, the goodness of

God is to the worshiping heart. To behold the beauty of the Lord is to experience him as the supremely desirable, delightful, and attractive.[33] As Jürgen Moltmann put it, "The beautiful in God is what makes us rejoice in him."[34] A.W. Tozer knew this same truth: "The blessed and inviting truth is that God is the most winsome of all beings, and in our worship of Him we should find unspeakable pleasure."[35] Do you know this beauty? Have you experienced this pleasure? It is glorious!

There is also the joy of discovering God's glory, or moral beauty, reflected in us. "And we all, with unveiled face, beholding the glory of the Lord, are being transformed into the same image from one degree of glory to another. For this comes from the Lord who is the Spirit."[36] We can't know the glory of God in life, enjoy his presence, delight in his beauty, and remain the same. A spiritual transformation takes place. His beauty gradually, by degree, becomes ours. Jonathan Edwards wrote:

> Another emanation of divine fulness, is the communication of virtue and *holiness* to the creature: this is a communication of God's holiness; so that hereby the creature partakes of God's own moral excellency; which is properly the beauty of the divine nature. And as God delights in his own beauty, he must necessarily delight in the creature's holiness; which is a conformity to and participation of it, as truly as a brightness of a jewel, held in the sun's beams, is a participation or derivation of the sun's brightness, though immensely less in degree.[37]

There is great joy here: an incredulous joy in becoming a stained-glass window through which God's glory shines, a surprised pleasure in becoming a tangible token of his presence in the world, a delight in being changed "from one degree of glory to another."[38]

A GREATER GLORY

If the apostle Paul is right (and I am confident that he is), there is greater glory in God's transformational work in us today than there was in the epic events that surrounded the giving of the law through Moses:

> Now if the ministry of death, carved in letters on stone, came with such *glory* that the Israelites could not gaze at Moses' face because of its *glory*, which was being brought to an end, will not the ministry of the Spirit have even more *glory*? For if there was *glory* in the ministry of condemnation, the ministry of righteousness must far exceed it in *glory*. . . . For if what was being brought to an end came with *glory*, much more will what is permanent have *glory*. . . . Now the Lord is the Spirit, and where the Spirit of the Lord is, there is freedom. And we all, with unveiled face, *beholding the glory of the Lord*, are being transformed into the same image *from one degree of glory to another*. For this comes from the Lord who is the Spirit. (2 Corinthians 3:7-18)

To know the presence and work of the Spirit is to know the glory of God. It may not seem as dramatic as the theophanies of the Old Testament, but it is not at all inferior. That we can think otherwise means only that we don't know what we are talking about. Paul saw the truth undimmed: The life-transforming presence and power of the Spirit is a greater glory than the extraordinary light that transformed the countenance of Moses.[39]

In this era of the Spirit, the glory of God in its most significant mode does not impinge upon our senses, but upon our hearts. But it is no less the glory of God for that! Paul was struck blind when his eyes beheld the glory of the risen Christ on the road to Damascus.[40] But he also claimed that allbelievers encounter the "glory of God in the face of Christ" shining in their hearts.[41] It is the same Christ and the same glory.

The earth is full of God's glory,[42] but so is our joy.[43] Joy betokens the presence of God no less than the beauty and wonders of nature,[44] or shafts of light appearing from no visible source. In the inner work of the Spirit we truly behold the glory of the Lord,[45] and in that gaze of the heart, we discover another dimension of our joy. This does not minimize the glory of God in the world; it exalts his glory in our hearts. The first is very great, the second even greater.

GOD'S GLORY IN CHRIST

If glory is a cut gem, God's glory in Christ is its largest and most lustrous facet. Jesus is the brightest and clearest of all the ways that God has made himself known. We find our greatest joy in him:

> Long ago, at many times and in many ways, God spoke to our fathers by the prophets, but in these last days he has spoken to us by his Son, whom he appointed the heir of all things, through whom also he created the world. *He is the radiance of the glory of God* and the exact imprint of his nature. (Hebrews 1:1-2)

> And the Word became flesh and dwelt among us, and *we have seen his glory, glory as of the only Son from the Father,* full of grace and truth. . . . No one has ever seen God; the only God, who is at the Father's side, he has made him known. (John 1:14, 18)

> The god of this world has blinded the minds of the unbelievers, to keep them from seeing the light of the gospel of *the glory of Christ, who is the image of God.* (2 Corinthians 4:4)

How do we connect with this glory when we have never seen Jesus? First, let me hold out to you the prospect that it is entirely possible, even in our day: "Though you have not seen him, you love him. Though you do not now see him, you believe in him and rejoice with joy that is inexpressible and filled with glory."[46]

There is a Gospel story about Jesus that we have come to know as "The Transfiguration." As soon as you read it you will recognize it as a story of glory:

> [Jesus] took Peter, John and James with him and went up onto a mountain to pray. As he was praying, the appearance of his face changed, and his clothes became as bright as a flash of lightning. Two men, Moses and Elijah, appeared in *glorious splendor*, talking with Jesus. They spoke about his departure, which he was about to bring to fulfillment at Jerusalem. Peter and his companions were very sleepy, but when they became fully awake, *they saw his glory* and the two men standing with him. As the men were leaving Jesus, Peter said to him, "Master, it is good for us to be here. Let us put up three shelters—one for you, one for Moses and one for Elijah." (He did not know what he was saying.) While he was speaking, a cloud appeared and covered them, and they were afraid as they entered the cloud. A voice came from the cloud, saying, "This is my Son, whom I have chosen; listen to him." (Luke 9:28-36, NIV)

This is a classic Divine Visitation: an incursion of the supernatural, a bright luminosity with no earthly source, a cloud, and an uncanny, otherworldly voice. I would have been frightened and bewildered, too!

But this is much more than classic. It is the Divine Visitation *par excellence*.[47] This glory eclipses the glory of all Visitations before it.[48] Glory envelopes Jesus, transforming his countenance with brilliant light. *Postmortem*, Moses and Elijah appear in "glorious splendor." And then God himself speaks from a cloud. Years later this event would be celebrated in these words:

> For we did not follow cleverly devised stories when we told you about the coming of our Lord Jesus Christ in power, but *we were eyewitnesses of his majesty*. He received honor and *glory* from God

the Father when the voice came to him from *the Majestic Glory*, saying, "This is my Son, whom I love; with him I am well pleased." We ourselves heard this voice that came from heaven when we were with him on the sacred mountain. (2 Peter 1:16-18, NIV)

How do we come to know God's glory in his Son? By embracing what God says about him. As there were in the first century, there are many opinions about who Jesus is in our day.[49] But there is only one judgment that matters: God's, and he declares to us, "This is my Son." Here is the mystery and wonder of the Incarnation. In Jesus, God himself has come among us: "And the Word became flesh and dwelt among us, and *we have seen his glory, glory as of the only Son from the Father*, full of grace and truth."[50] This is where the glory is.

God's Word to us is not only that Jesus is his Son, but that he is chosen by God, beloved to God, the one in whom God delights. These are ways of describing the Messiah foretold by the prophets:

> Behold my servant, whom I uphold,
>   my chosen, in whom my soul delights;
> I have put my Spirit upon him;
>   he will bring forth justice to the nations. (Isaiah 42:1; compare
>   Matthew 12:17-18)

To know God's glory in Christ, we must receive and affirm God's Word about him. He must be the Son of God *to us*, the Messiah *to us*, God's chosen and beloved *to us*, the one in whom *we* delight. And then, because he is all of this, we welcome God's word to us: "Listen to him." We cultivate a hunger and thirst for the words of Jesus. We treasure them above all other words. We believe his teaching. We obey his commands. We trust his promises. This is where the glory is. This is where we discover joy.

QUESTIONS FOR THOUGHT AND DISCUSSION

1. What can you do to cultivate a sense of God's glory in the world? In what ways can you deepen and expand your joy in God's glory in the world?

   Spend More time... time in Nature...

2. If you know someone who venerates nature, and sees it as somehow divine, how would you go about introducing him or her to God's glory in nature, and how this is different and far greater?

   pray... James 1:5
   Sarah· reasoning about Plato

3. Have you ever experienced a Divine Visitation? How would you describe your openness to that possibility in your life? What difference does this make to your understanding of God?

   Yes - In bed, praying For Daniel. A deep, Audible voice within... "He will be o.k."

4. How can you put this Psalm into practice in your life? What would it look like?

   > O my Strength, I will watch for you,
   >> for you, O God, are my fortress.
   > My God in his steadfast love will meet me. (Psalm 59:8-9)

   Intentionally drawing my eyes towards God, recognizing His love for me, and being in community

5. What are the implications of the Transfiguration for your understanding of Jesus? How does it affect your relationship with him?

   c Him all day!

CHAPTER 3

Spend More time.... time In Nature....

JOY AND GOD'S WORLD

prad ... James 1:5
Sarah- reasoning about Plato

O nce upon a time, or before there was time, there was God, and only
God. Then he created. He sang a pure and powerful song, and
suddenly angels surrounded his throne. Myriads of heavenly creatures.
Countless ranks. As they joined his song, lending harmony to the Maker's
creative melody, galaxies and stars and planets, billions upon billions, came
into existence.[1] And then his musical mandate brought forth a particular
world, our own, filled with plants, insects, and animals – sea-swimmers,
land-walkers, and sky-flyers – as many and varied as the luminaries in the
night sky. Nearly finished, he sang once more and fashioned the crown of
his handiwork, humans – a man and a woman – to mirror him in his world,
and to steward and rule it in his stead.

Why did God create? The answer can't be that he was lonely or bored,
that it was a whim or an inadvertence, that he was somehow compelled to
do it, or that there was a deficit in his existence that could only be remedied
by creating a universe. None of this can be true of the Supreme Being.[2]
God's life was full and complete before he spoke the first word of creation.
This is the right answer to our question: God created from the plenitude of

his pleasure. He created from the overflow of his joy.[3] It was his pleasure to create; it is ours that he did.

God is not only joyful beyond imagination, he generous beyond words.[4] If we rejoice in him, we are also invited to enjoy his gifts. He welcomes us to delight in the things he has made – which makes our joy as high as the heavens and as wide as the world.

Joy is first and foremost our enjoyment of God, but he intends our joy in him to include the world he has made.[5]   Pleasures of the earth are not meant to rival our joy in God, but to enlarge and enrich our experience of his goodness. He takes pleasure in what he has made, and invites us to do so as well:

> May the glory of the LORD endure forever;
>   may the LORD rejoice in his works. (Psalm 104:31)
>
> At the works of your hands I sing for joy. (Psalm 92:4)
>
> Great are the works of the LORD, studied by all who delight in them. (Psalm 111:2)
>
> The godly, wheresoever they cast their eyes, beholding heaven and earth, the air and water, see and acknowledge all for God's wonders; and, full of astonishment and delight, laud the Creator, knowing that God is well pleased therewith.[6]

Creation expands the arena of our joy. It is meant to include not only our Maker, but his world. God intends our joy to be a celebration of his joy in his handiwork and the pleasure of being beneficiaries of his overflowing generosity.

THE EARTH IS FULL OF HIS GLORY!

The enjoyment of the world is more than the enjoyment of the world. It is an encounter with the One who made the world, is everywhere present in it, and reveals himself through it. If you delight in the beauty of a rainbow, you are not merely observing a refraction of light through moisture in the air; you are beholding the colorful glory of God. If you have ever huddled in your house as the night sky was ripped by bolts of lightning and thunder shook your bones, you witnessed more than an electrical storm; you came face to face with the raucous glory of God. If you've ever felt dwarfed as you walked through a rivered canyon, with peaks towering to the heavens around you, you experienced more than your smallness in a very big world; you were humbled by the immense glory of God.

There is more to the world than the world itself. In the words of Peter Kreeft, "There is something bigger than the world out there hiding behind everything in the world, and our chief joy is with it."[7] Our chief joy is with God himself, present in, and revealing himself through, all that we encounter in the world:

> Holy, holy, holy is the LORD of hosts;
>> the whole earth is full of his glory. (Isaiah 6:3)

> Do I not fill heaven and earth? declares the LORD.
> (Jeremiah 23:24)

> The heavens declare the glory of God,
>> and the sky above proclaims his handiwork.
> Day to day pours out speech,
>> and night to night reveals knowledge.
> There is no speech, nor are there words,
>> whose voice is not heard.
> Their voice goes out through all the earth,
>> and their words to the end of the world. (Psalm 19:1-4)

You should turn . . . to a living God who made the heaven and the earth and the sea and all that is in them. In past generations he allowed all the nations to walk in their own ways; yet he did not leave himself without witness, for he did good and by giving you from heaven rains and fruitful seasons, satisfying your hearts with food and gladness. (Acts 14:15-17)[8]

God is not another name for nature. He is not it. He is Other. That is his transcendence. He is neither identical to, nor bound by, his creation. Nevertheless, he fills it. He is everywhere present in it, from the inner life of an atom to the outer reaches of the farthest galaxies. Wherever you turn he is there, behind and before, on either side, above and below, and deep within.[9] His sovereign power and animating presence orders and sustains life in every moment and in every place. That is his immanence.[10]

The presence of God in creation is intangible, but the *tokens* of his presence are not. They are constantly presented to us as divine revelation. In fact we cannot escape them, even if are unaware of them.[11] They surround us at all times as his glory filling the earth, as the many and varied manifestations of the invisible, ubiquitous God. This includes the pleasures of the world. C.S. Lewis saw it truly: "I was learning the far more secret doctrine that *pleasures* are shafts of the glory as it strikes our sensibility. As it impinges on our will or our understanding, we give it different names – goodness or truth or the like. But its flash upon our senses and mood is pleasure."[12] Pleasure whispers the goodness of God to us.[13] It sings his love for us. It is a splash of his overflowing joy.

A WORLD FOR US

Why did God create? Because it was his joy to do so. Why did he create a world of beauty and fragrances and textures and sounds, and sentient creatures like us to inhabit it? For our joy. All the wonders and pleasures of creation are meant for us. Luther saw this truth clearly:

> Our loving Lord God will that we eat, drink, and be merry, making use of his creatures, *for therefore he created them.* He will not that we complain, as if he had not given sufficient, or that he could not maintain our poor carcasses; he asks only that we acknowledge him for our God, and thank him for his gifts.[14]

Calvin concurred: "The Lord himself, by the very order of creation, has demonstrated that he created all things *for the sake of man.*"[15] In our own day Nicholas Wolterstorff has written: "When the Christian affirms the goodness of the physical creation, he is not just praising its magnificence. He is saying that the physical creation is good *for human beings.* It serves human fulfillment."[16]

When we affirm the truths of creation, it is not enough to say that God created, or even that what he created is good. God created, all of his creation is good, and all of it is meant for us. The apostle Paul did not retreat from this startling notion:

> All things are yours . . . the world or life or death or the present or the future — all are yours. (1 Corinthians 3:21-22).

> Everything created by God is good, and nothing is to be rejected if it is received with thanksgiving. (1 Timothy 4:4)

> [God] richly provides us with everything to enjoy. (1 Timothy 6:17)

This does not give us license to indulge selfish desires, but liberty to celebrate the goodness of God's world, and the rightness of our pleasure in it. It was given for our joy, and, through our thankful enjoyment of it, to reflect the beneficence of our God. Arthur Holmes was right: "If God's creation has value, then the enjoyment of its benefits can celebrate God's goodness. All of life, in fact, becomes just such a celebration – provided one recognizes the one who made it so heartily good."[17]

THE SACRED SECRET

C.S. Lewis wrote, God "likes matter. He invented it."[18] He created the heavens and the earth and then made corporeal beings to inhabit them. Of all the worlds he might have brought into being, he chose this one with all of its tangible properties.

Matter is God's invention, and pleasure is his gift. God created us not only to steward his world, but to savor it. The physical world, our senses, and minds that transcend and appreciate sentient experience point to something greater than themselves. They bear witness to the Creator's design for pleasure. There is something mysterious and wonderful here! Pleasures are "the faint, far-off results of those energies which God's creative rapture implanted in matter."[19] We seriously misunderstand matter and seriously mistake pleasure if we don't see them in relation to the Creator and his good and wise design for us.

Pleasure as we know it is not only sacred by virtue of its divine origin and blessing, it is a gift that is ours alone. In the words of Pascal, we are neither angels nor brutes.[20] Lacking bodies, angels are incapable of experiencing the sensory dimension of pleasure. Lacking our cognitive abilities, brutes are strangers to its appreciative dimension. Angels may know reflective delights, and animals, pleasurable stimuli, but only we can enjoy them both, and enjoy them in the same experience. It is unique to us. We profane our pleasures when we treat them as less than sacred. We diminish them when we do not delight in them as the "secret that . . . [God] has shared with us alone."[21]

CREATION, FALL, AND REDEMPTION

I can guess what you are thinking, and you are right. All of this sounds too Edenic. It doesn't reckon with the Fall and the effect of sin upon the world and our affections.[22] After all, the Bible says some pretty negative things about the pursuit of pleasure.[23] We can't simply affirm pleasure without qualification in our world. Augustine saw the problem clearly:

> Within also, within is another evil, arising out of the same kind of temptation; whereby they become empty who please themselves in themselves . . . . But in pleasing themselves, they much displease You, not merely taking pleasure in things not good, as if they were good, but in Your good things as though they were their own; or even as if in Yours, yet as though of their own merits; or even if as though of Your grace, yet not with friendly rejoicings . . . .[24]

Lewis saw this perversion of pleasure at the very heart of the Fall: "Someone or something whispered that they could become as gods – that they could cease directing their lives to their Creator and taking all their delights as uncovenanted mercies . . . which arose in the course of a life directed not to those delights but to the adoration of God."[25]

Does our sinful state make delight in the world's pleasures a bad thing? Some Christians have thought so. For them, pleasures that are unnecessary for personal survival or the continuation of the human race should be shunned. The few that are indispensable to those ends, like eating and procreation, are necessary evils, permitted as sparingly as possible, with a sense of embarrassment and even shame that we must make concessions to them.

I can't believe that this is what God intends for us! It is not the world, but worldliness, that is evil — treating the pleasures of the world as ends in themselves. It is not sensory experience, but sensualism, that is evil — treating pleasure as if it defined the meaning of our lives.

Good is so much more powerful than evil (because God is so much more powerful than his adversaries) that the fallenness of our world cannot negate the goodness of God's gifts to us in creation. Faced with ascetics in his day who urged abstinence from marriage and certain foods, the apostle Paul labeled their teaching "doctrines of demons," and "hypocrisy," and those who advocated it "liars seared in their own consciences as with a branding iron."[26] His antidote for such error? Affirming the goodness of God's creation even in a fallen world. The pleasures of marriage and food are good gifts "which God has created to be gratefully shared in by those who believe and know the truth. For everything created by God is good, and nothing is to be rejected, if it is received with gratitude: for it is sanctified by means of the word of God and prayer."[27]

C.S. Lewis wrote:

> But aren't there bad, unlawful pleasures? Certainly there are. But in calling them "bad pleasures" I take it we are using a kind of shorthand. We mean "pleasures" snatched by unlawful acts." It is the stealing of the apple that is bad, not the sweetness. The sweetness is still a beam from the glory. That does not palliate the stealing. It makes it worse. There is a sacrilege in the theft. We have abused a holy thing. . . .[28]

Sin has spoiled much that is good about pleasure, but this is an indictment of us, and not of pleasure itself. The gift is still good; it is our desecration of it that is evil.

A Christian approach to pleasure will be shaped by the truths of Creation, Fall, and Redemption: meeting pleasure first with affirmation and celebration because all that God creates is good, then with a sober reckoning of sin and its ramifications, and finally with joyous reaffirmation, as the gifts of creation are reclaimed through the redemptive work of Christ and are restored to the Creator's good intentions for us.[29]

For some Christians, Redemption counters the Fall, but is irrelevant to Creation. Grace saves us from our sin, but has little to do with the heavens and the earth and our place in them. This is seriously incomplete, and seriously mistaken as a result! Redemption remedies the Fall and reclaims Creation. In fact, one day Creation will be raised to greater heights in the new heavens and the new earth, and the resurrection of our bodies.[30] The final state of the redeemed will not be an incorporeal mode of existence in a spirit-world, but glorified physical life in a newly created world whose wonders will far surpass those of Eden. The apostle Paul wrote of this:

> For the creation was subjected to futility, not willingly, but because of him who subjected it, in hope that the creation itself will be set free from its bondage to corruption and obtain the freedom of the glory of the children of God. For we know that the whole creation has been groaning together in the pains of childbirth until now. And not only the creation, but we ourselves who have the firstfruits of the Spirit, groan inwardly as we wait eagerly for adoption as sons, the redemption of our bodies. (Romans 8:20-23)

In the present, we must affirm the world, forsake it, and then enjoy it anew as a taste of God's goodness and a foretaste of the glories that await us in the new heavens and the new earth.[31]

PLEASURE AND THE RENEWING OF OUR MINDS

Our minds play an important role in our experience of pleasure.[32] Consider aesthetic pleasure. Augustine wrote: "There is no corporeal beauty, whether in the condition of a body, as figure, or in its movement, as in music, of which it is not *the mind* that judges."[33] According to Aquinas, "Beauty relates to the *cognitive* faculty."[34] Closer to our own day, David Elton Trueblood wrote, "In the appreciation of beauty the physical senses are involved, but they are by no means sufficient to the aesthetic result. Always there is a *process of thought*."[35]

Not only do our minds assess properties like proportion, form, and unity, they make the summary judgment that something is beautiful, and invite our affections to respond in enjoyment. This is the truth behind the saying, "Beauty is in the eye of the beholder." Not so much in the eye as in the mind.

What is true of aesthetic pleasure is true, in nuanced ways, of all pleasures. They are never merely experienced, they are construed. In fact, the interpretation of a pleasure is integral to the pleasure itself. C.S. Lewis wrote:

> We can't – or I can't – hear the song of a bird simply as a sound. Its meaning or message ("That's a bird") comes with it inevitably – just as one can't see a familiar word in print as a merely visual pattern. The reading is as involuntary as the seeing. When the wind roars I don't just hear the roar; I "hear the wind." In the same way it is possible to "read" as well as to "have" a pleasure. Or not even "as well as." The distinction ought to become, and sometimes is, impossible; to receive it and to recognise its divine source are a single experience. This heavenly fruit is instantly redolent of the orchard where it grew. This sweet air whispers of the country from

whence it blows. It is a message. We know we are being touched by a finger of that right hand at which there are pleasures for evermore. There need be no question of thanks or praise as a separate event, something done afterwards. To experience the tiny theophany is itself to adore.[36]

To *have* a pleasure and to *read* its divine Source ought to be, and can be, a single experience. The problem is that this doesn't happen automatically in our fallen state. For those in whom the Spirit of God is not at work, it doesn't seem to happen at all. They *have* the pleasure and *read* its significance apart from God. Pagan pleasure is a form of idolatry: It is wrongly construed, its Source is never honored, and the Giver is never thanked. It is sacrilege: stripping pleasure of its sacred dimensions and treating it as something profane.

If our pleasures are out of step with God's intention for them, whatever else may be the case, our thinking has gone wrong. When the apostle Paul indicted his generation for its perversion of pleasure, this is how he described the guilty parties:

[They] suppress the truth.

[They became] futile in their thinking.

[Their] foolish hearts were darkened.

Claiming to be wise, they became fools.

[They] exchanged the truth about God for a lie.

God gave them up to a debased mind. [37]

In our fallen state, there is perversion in c
delights. The dispositions of our hearts
disordered. Our thoughts are disoriented. Th
good news: This can be redeemed! Luther wro

> Nature, which is corrupted by original s
> without abuse the things created and given
> this is the nature of created things but be   ...t of him
> who uses them is evil. But if the heart has been reformed by the
> Spirit, it makes use of both the useful and the delightful things in a
> holy manner and with thanksgiving.[38]

Redemption brings about a radical change as we are "transformed by the renewing of our minds."[39] Pleasure is consecrated as truth is embraced, and the fruits of creation are received with thankful prayer. It is worth returning to the words of Paul: "God created [marriage and food] to be received with thanksgiving by those who believe and know the truth. For everything created by God is good, and nothing is to be rejected if it is received with thanksgiving, for it is made holy by the word of God and prayer."[40]

Here pleasure approaches its divine intention as a sign of God's presence in the world and a taste of his goodness. As our minds become habituated in a God-framed-and-centered-way-of-seeing-life, and we grow in conviction and confidence in this vision, not only do we find the sting removed from our hardships, we discover a greater joy in all that is positive and pleasurable in life.

It is important for us to affirm Creation and the Fall, acknowledging both the goodness of pleasure and our perversion of pleasure. Neither is the last word on the matter, however. The last word is Redemption, where the effects of the Fall are countered, and the bounty of Creation is consecrated

...ken of God's goodness to us, and a sign that points our
...onders of the new heavens and earth that await us.

JOYFUL STEWARDS

If we look at the world through the lens of joy we will see God in all that we behold. In its vastness we will see his immensity. In its great antiquity we will see his eternal power. In its grandeur we will see his glory. In its wonders we will see his wisdom. In its intricacies we will see his genius. In its wildness we will see his sovereign freedom and surprising ways. In its pleasures we will see his goodness to us. If we see the world as it truly is, we will see it enchanted with the presence of God.[41]

If our first response to the world is anything but reverence, wonder, and awe, we haven't seen it truly. We are out of touch with reality. There is much that we will miss and much that we will misuse because we misunderstand the true nature and significance of the world. We will live in it like witless thugs throwing fine crystal into the air for target practice.

Our first calling as bearers of God's image is to enjoy and steward the earth as a theater for his glory.[42] We should do nothing to diminish it. Nothing to disgrace it. Nothing to sully it. Nothing to spoil it. We should do everything we can to protect it. Everything we can to preserve it. We should use but not abuse. We should enjoy but not exploit. Because it bears the presence of God, the earth is sacred. Because it is a habitation of God, it is holy. Our stewardship must begin here.

Our responsibility to steward the earth includes managing its resources for the good of humanity. God does not intend that some (who happen to have and control wealth) should enjoy the benefits of his world and others (who do not) should not. Nor does he intend that one generation should tap the resources of his world in a way that deprives future generations of them.[43] It isn't our planet. We don't have that right:

The earth is the LORD's and the fullness thereof,
　　the world and those who dwell therein. (Psalm 24:1)

One generation shall laud your works to another,
　　and shall declare your mighty acts. (Psalm 145:4)

It should come as no surprise that our stewardship of the earth is meant to reflect the two great commandments we have been given: to love God fully and supremely, and to love our neighbors as ourselves.[44] We are called to manage the resources of the world as an expression of love for its Maker and ours. We are called to steward its stores as an expression of love for our neighbor – near and far, present and future.

Now, our challenge as people who must live with their feet on the ground is how to pursue these things when so many care so little. What difference can we make when governments and corporations – power brokers who control, consume, and often contaminate the resources of the world – reject and even revile a true vision of God's world? Jesus would tell us that they must be included in our daily prayer:

Our Father in heaven,
hallowed be your name.
Your kingdom come,
your will be done,
　　on earth as it is in heaven. (Matthew 6:9-10)

The desecration and despoiling of God's world, and the unjust distribution of its resources, are spiritual problems. Until hearts are aligned with God's, and knees bow to his rightful dominion, there is little hope for a better world.

Whatever governments and private enterprises may say or do, there is a higher government to which we must answer, and a greater enterprise to which we have been enlisted. As far as it lies with us we should steward the earth for the glory of God and the good of others, and revel in the joy God gives as we do this. Then, to all who will listen, in our words and by our deeds, let us proclaim the truths of Creation and the joys of stewardship, and pray heartily that many more will join us!

QUESTIONS FOR THOUGHT AND DISCUSSION

1. Daniel MaGuire has written, "Biblical joy is not a gossamer strain of otherworldly spirituality; it is of the earth and earthy." As you reflect on your view of joy before reading this chapter, would you characterize it as "otherworldly spirituality" or "of the earth and earthy"? Identify the factors that shaped your view.

2. How does God's joy in creation influence your view of the world?

3. Discuss the following quote from the chapter. Have you had similar experiences? How have they impacted your understanding of God?

> The enjoyment of the world is more than the enjoyment of the world. It is an encounter with the One who made the world, is everywhere present in it, and reveals himself through it. If you delight in the beauty of a rainbow, you are not merely observing a refraction of light through moisture in the air; you are beholding the colorful glory of God. If you have ever huddled in your house as the night sky was ripped by bolts of lightning and thunder shook your bones, you witnessed more than an electrical storm; you came face to face with the raucous glory of God. If you've ever felt dwarfed as you walked through a rivered canyon, with peaks towering to the heavens around you, you experienced more than your smallness in a very big world; you were humbled by the immense glory of God.

4. "Pleasure is consecrated as truth is embraced, and the fruits of creation are received with thankful prayer." What would this look like as a daily practice for you?

5. How can you take the section "'Joyful Stewards" into conversations with your peers about environmental ethics and issues of global economics and justice?

CHAPTER 4

THE JOY OF SALVATION

I f I could travel through history and visit any time and place in the world, after first century Palestine in the days of Jesus my destination would be the Garden of Eden before the human rebellion that took place there. Have you ever wondered why we are given no more than a tantalizing glimpse of Edenic life in the Sacred Word? I don't know the answer, of course. Perhaps God chose not to let us see more of that world because it would break our hearts and cripple our will to live in our own. Only he knows.

Sometimes my heart aches for Eden. For that ancient *garden of delights.*[1] I long for the world God first created. A world unspoiled and unsullied by sin. A world filled with tokens of the divine Presence, from the shimmering light of stars overhead to the cool, crystalline dew beneath one's feet at the dawning of the day, each and every one pointing vividly and irresistibly to its Source. I yearn for the world in which the knowledge of God was untrammeled, and every blink of the eye brought one into touch with some new dimension of his glory. I long for the day long past when no distinction was even possible between sensual and spiritual, when all pleasures were joyful, directed to God in thanksgiving and praise, and joy pulsed with pleasure in the Creator and the good world that he created.[2]

JOY LOST

Alas, that world did not survive. Perhaps it could not have. Its brevity is linked to the mystery of human freedom. The unthinkable happened. Our forebears chose the pleasure of the Creator's good gifts over the Creator himself. They chose to forge their own future rather than embrace the adventures God had in store for them. They chose to write their own story rather than play a part in God's. Though it was sheer folly to do so, they turned their will away from the will of God. The harmony between Being and being was destroyed. Real pleasures were lost, and sensual idols took their place. The joy that bound creature to creature and all created things to the Creator became a wistful memory. A whisper that few still hear, beckoning the heart to a better time and a better world.

Why did God make us free? Look at what we have done with our freedom! C.S. Lewis was right:

> God created things which had free will. That means creatures which can go either wrong or right. Some people think they can imagine a creature which was free but had no possibility of going wrong; I cannot. If a thing is free to be good it is also free to be bad. And free will is what has made evil possible. Why, then, did God give them free will? Because free will, though it makes evil possible, is also the only thing that makes possible any love or goodness or joy worth having. A world of automata -- of creatures that worked like machines -- would hardly be worth creating. *The happiness which God designs for His higher creatures is the happiness of being freely, voluntarily united to Him and to each other in an ecstasy of love and delight compared with which the most rapturous love between a man and a woman on this earth is mere milk and water. And for that they must be free.*[3]

Our freedom made joy possible. Our misuse of that gift shattered the fragile and precious jewel. Only shards remain, bits and pieces strewn over the sands of human experience like the remains of a long-lost and once-glorious civilization.

What great loss the Fall brought to our race!

We are used to living with our sin, like skunks at home with their own stench. We take as normal fare what the Bible treats as a great horror and scandal.[4] Nothing could be more abnormal than humanity in its fallen condition. Nothing more unnatural. In our sinful state we have exchanged the glory of God for smudgy little gods of our own making, and the wine of joy for the waste of our own perversions: an obscene draught, which, though it offends the sensibilities of heaven, we have come absurdly to prefer.

The Bible declares: "Those who choose another god multiply their sorrows."[5] To limit this to images of wood and stone is to miss the point. To make a god of anything other than the living and true God is to forsake the Fountain of Joy.[6] It is to drink instead from the fetid marshes of our own folly. Idols of the heart are not only tokens of defiance, but monuments to our insanity. The self-inflicted wounds of idolatry, in fact, are its greatest irony. Make a god of money and you will pierce your heart with many pangs.[7] Make a god of pleasure and you may as well try to grasp the wind in your hands.[8] Whatever our god, at whatever self-made shrine we bow, we forgo by that choice the joy for which we were created, and embrace a course that will lead only to sorrow beyond anything we can imagine. As Peter Kreeft put it, "Since an idol *is* not God, no matter how sincerely or passionately it is treated as God, it is bound to break the heart of the worshipper, sooner or later . . . . You can't get blood from a stone or divine joy from nondivine things."[9]

The temptation our first parents faced was to become like God.[10] They were enticed to leave their station under the gracious and sovereign rule of

God and to grasp at something they foolishly believed would be better. They sought a greater good; they found, instead, a Curse: alienation from the Creator, from themselves, from each other, and from all other creature-life. They made themselves petty deities, and, in that choice, multiplied their sorrow. Day after day brought forth new grief, from the painful memory of Eden-lost to the horrors of their own growing evil. It is an ancient story. Every chapter tells much the same tale. Only the times, places, and characters change. We are all sons of Adam and daughters of Eve. We have all shared in their sin and know their consequent sorrow.

This is the condition of fallen humanity. This is what it means to be "by nature children of wrath."[11] The wrath of God is not a bolt of lighting, thrown Zeus-like from the heavens to punish wrongdoers. *Wrath is joy rejected.*[12] Peter Kreeft is right: "But the opposite of true joy is far worse than anguish . . . . In fact, its opposite is hell."[13] Jesus' description of perdition is no pre-scientific fiction. It is as realistic as anything can be. Hell is a place of weeping and gnashing of teeth.[14] Ultimate sorrow and grief. If joy is found only in the undimmed presence of God,[15] and hell is the darkness of eternal separation from him,[16] there is no other way that it could be. Hell is the place of divine wrath: joy refused and forfeited with finality. It is the unending, unmitigated sorrow of choosing another god.[17] It became one of two destinies the day our first parents took their first steps from the Garden.[18]

JOY REGAINED

Fallen earth is neither Eden nor hell. Sin accounts for the first, and grace for the second. Short of hell, joy lost can be regained. In fact, this is the heart of our redemption.

The joy of God in salvation. The joy of salvation begins with the joy of the Savior.[19] Our joy, here, as everywhere, is sourced in the overflowing joy of God. His mercy is not meager, his goodness never grudging. It is lavish.

Profuse. A cascading waterfall. A coursing river. A fathomless, brimming well. A thirst-quenching drink poured into the dry and desolate hearts of men and women in desperate need of spiritual refreshment.[20]

Why did God become one of us in Jesus of Nazareth? The Nicene Creed answers this with the words, "For us human beings and for our salvation."[21] Our sin and misery created the need for God's action in Christ. But there is another question we can ask: Why would God do this?[22] Our need did not create an obligation for him. He could have left us in our sin and been fully just in doing so. Why did he not only script the drama of salvation, but in Christ step onto the stage of human history as its central character? Because it was his joy to do so.

With a sense of wonder the prophet Micah asked, "Who is a God like you, pardoning iniquity and passing over transgression?" No one! This is astonishing! Not at all what sinners should expect from a holy God! But there is an even greater wonder when we ask why God would deal with us so. Micah's answer takes us to the heart of God: "because he delights in steadfast love."[23] There is unimaginable pleasure here that only God can know. This insight into God's heart leapt to life in the assuring words of Jesus: "Fear not, little flock, for it is the Father's good pleasure to give you the kingdom."[24] And, "Just so, I tell you there is . . . joy in heaven over one sinner who repents" (a joy pictured in the parable with music, dancing and a great feast).[25]

The author of Hebrews wrote of Jesus: "For the joy that was set before him [he] endured the cross, despising the shame, and is seated at the right hand of the throne of God."[26] This joy was not merely the anticipation of future glory and his exaltation at the right hand of the Father. It was the joy of "bringing many children to glory," passing through death to "destroy the one who has the power of death, that is, the devil," and to "free those who all their lives were held in slavery by the fear of death."[27] It was the vision of his redemptive work completed in us and for us that brought him such joy, even in the hour of his greatest suffering and pain. So great was Christ's joy in bringing salvation to a sinful world that even the agony of the Cross was compelled to yield to it. If we cannot fathom his passion (and we cannot), we will never plumb his greater pleasure in its outcome. Nevertheless, our joy in salvation begins here. Our boon in redemption lies in the bountiful joy of our Redeemer.

Our joy in salvation. God enjoys bringing salvation to sinners, and sinners to salvation. It is a joy for him to renovate our hearts, opening them to all he has done for us, all that he is now doing, and all that he has pledged to do.[28] This transformation begins with the birth of something radically new within us. Jesus described it as being born again, born from above, born of the Spirit.[29] The apostle Paul put it in these words: "Therefore, if any one is in Christ, he is a new creation; the old has passed away, behold, the new has come."[30] This conversion from death to life is not something we do or could possibly bring about. It is the work of God, revolutionizing our innermost being and freeing us to live from a transformed heart. It is the genesis of our joy. A.W. Tozer wrote, "The very moment that the Spirit of God has quickened us to His life in regeneration, our whole being senses its kinship to God and leaps up in joyous recognition."[31] Our initiation into the joy of salvation lies here.

When grace triumphs in us, we come to revel in our need for God. Our plight brings us pleasure.[32] We experience grace as a feast offered to poor, famished, thirsty wayfarers a step away from perishing in their desperate want:

> Ho everyone who thirsts,
>   come to the waters;
> and you that have no money,
>   come, buy and eat!

Come, buy wine and milk
    without money and without price.
Why do you spend your money for that which is not bread,
    and your labor for that which does not satisfy?
Listen carefully to me, and eat what is good,
    and delight yourselves in rich food.
Incline your ear, and come to me;
    listen so that you may live. (Isaiah 55:1-3, NRSV)

In our sin we are utterly lost and ruined, without hope because we fully deserve the trouble we are in and can do nothing to change it. Nothing to escape it. We cannot see a light, and could not move toward it even if we did. Sin brings only unrelenting darkness and despair. And then. And then God. And then God transforms our troubled lot. He pardons us! Rescues us! Delivers us! He reaches down to us when we could not reach up to him. He meets us in our misery. He sings to us, sings over us, and puts his song within us. We are enchanted by the music. He washes away the filth that caked us. Mends our brokenness. Dresses and heals our wounds. Clothes our nakedness in robes that befit royalty. Fills our aching and empty souls. Quenches our terrible thirst. Then, to our utter amazement, he invites us into an "ecstasy of love and delight," C.S. Lewis wrote, "compared with which the most rapturous love between a man and a woman on this earth is mere milk and water."[33] Hands that covered our face in shame now lift in grateful praise, and we join Mary's song: "My soul magnifies the Lord, and my spirit rejoices in God my Savior!"[34]

The joy of salvation is a restoration of joy in the Triune God. It is not the kind of joy we experience in viewing a sunset or a meadow of alpine flowers. It is more like the gaiety of a wedding dance: delighting in one's beloved and the celebration of love and life together. The joy of salvation is a participation in God's joy: the Father's joy in the Son and the Spirit, the Son's joy in the Father and the Spirit, the Spirit's joy in the Father and the Son, and the shared joy of the Three-in-One. Sin destroyed the communion of joy our kind once shared with this Three-Personal God.[35] Redemption restores it. We are brought back to, and drawn into, this Fellowship, or Dance, of joy. Joy is then experienced in its highest and purest form as love's delight: joy in God's Triune love for us, our small, growing love offered back to the Father, Son, and Holy Spirit, and the love and joy we share with all who have entered into the life of God.[36]

Eschatological joy. Joy is not only a memory of what our race once knew (a dormant memory waiting to be awakened), it is a foretaste of what we will one day know without measure or end. Words falter in our attempt to describe it. Jonathan Edwards saw this joy as "exceeding great and vigorous; impressing the heart with the most lively sensation of inexpressible sweetness, mightily moving, animating, and engaging . . . [us] *like a flame of fire.*"[37] C.S. Lewis described it differently:

> We are to be re-made. . . . [We shall discover what] we have never yet imagined: a real Man, an ageless god, a son of God, strong, radiant, wise, beautiful, and *drenched in joy.*[38]

> The faint far-off results of those energies which God's creative rapture implanted in matter when He made the worlds are what we now call physical pleasures; and even thus filtered, they are too much for our present management. What would it be to taste at the fountain-head that stream of which even these lower reaches prove so intoxicating? Yet that, I believe, is what lies before us. The whole man is to drink joy from the fountain of joy. As St. Augustine said, the rapture of the saved soul will "flow over" into the glorified body. In the light of our present specialized and depraved appetites we cannot imagine this *torrens voluptatus* [*river of pleasure*], and I warn everyone most seriously not to try.[39]

Is the joy of heaven a flaming fire or a river of pleasure? Will it warm us or drench us? We should not be surprised that the best Christian minds use conflicting metaphors to describe it. If our present joy can be "inexpressible and full of glory,"[40] human language is pressed beyond its limits to describe the joy that will far surpass anything we have yet experienced. (When Lewis warned us against trying to imagine it, he was seeking to spare us headache and heartache!)

The joy that awaits the people of God is not entirely future. Nor am I saying only that hoping for this future bliss strengthens our joy in the present.[41] I am saying, and truly mean it, that a dimension of our present joy is the joy of the age to come breaking back into human history in advance of its final consummation. It is ours now in an experience that is *partial, prospective,* and given to us in a *paradox.*

Our experience of this eschatological joy is *partial.* It is a "taste" of the "powers of the age to come."[42] The feast is future, but our taste of it in the present is no less real for that. The fruit of our present joy grows in the same orchard as heaven's joy. Jonathan Edwards wrote: "The love and joy of the saints on earth is the beginning and dawning of the light, life, and blessedness of heaven, and is like their love and joy there; or rather, the same in nature, though not the same in degree and circumstance."[43] Joy is one. Our experience may be partial, but joy itself cannot be parsed.

We still await the full and perfect realization of the Spirit's work, transforming our bodies and souls and fitting them for life in the age to come with its new heavens and new earth.[44] In the present, however, he is given to us as "the guarantee of our inheritance until we acquire possession of it."[45] We have received the first installment! It is not only a promise of what is still future to us, it is a realization of it in part. The Spirit's presence in our lives now is the "first fruits" of the full harvest that will come at the end of days.[46] It is a brand of fire from the blazing joy of the age to come. A splash from the river of pleasure in which we will one day be drenched.

Our experience of the joy of salvation is not only partial, it is *prospective*. By its very nature it anticipates. It points to the future, where it truly belongs and where it will be fully known.[47] The joy of salvation brings to us a poignant sense of being an alien in this fallen world, a misfit, a stranger, a pilgrim. The experience is both a presence and an absence of joy: The joy present delights our hearts, but the joy absent (because it is still future to us) creates a longing so powerful that it nearly breaks them. Its taste sharpens a hunger that will be fulfilled in what the Seer called the Marriage Feast of the Lamb:

> Let us rejoice and exult
>   and give him the glory,
> for the marriage of the Lamb has come,
>   and his Bride has made herself ready. (Revelation 19:7)
>
> Happy are those who are invited to the wedding supper of the Lamb. (Revelation 19:9)

Those who know this joy "desire a better country, that is, a heavenly one."[48] Their hearts yearn for their true homeland: the "city of God," with angels beyond count in "festal gathering."[49] They are both blessed and bereft until joy's consummation in the coming Kingdom.

Finally, the joy of salvation is given to us in a *paradox*, created by the fact that it is a taste of the "powers of the age to come"[50] while we still live in "the present evil age."[51] We are caught between two ages. We live "between the times," as George Eldon Ladd put it.[52] We are people who must daily embrace the dialectic of "already" and "not yet," of being "sorrowful, yet always rejoicing."[53] We experience something of the joy of the age to come even in the travail of this age. Peter captured this paradox as well as anyone:

> Blessed be the God and Father of our Lord Jesus Christ! By his great mercy we have been born anew to a living hope through the resurrection of Jesus Christ from the dead, and to an inheritance which is imperishable, undefiled, and unfading, kept in heaven for you, who by God's power are guarded through faith for a salvation ready to be revealed in the last time. In this you rejoice, though now for a little while you may have to suffer various trials." (1 Peter 1:3-6).

Both sides of the paradox must be affirmed and embraced. This age, in a death rattle, lingers; in Christ the age to come has broken back into the present in advance of its final consummation, bringing, in a preliminary way, the blessings and benefits of the "salvation ready to be revealed in the last time." Christian living is thus characterized by suffering (which belongs to this age) and the new birth (which belongs to the age to come). It is distinguished by a living hope and an undaunted joy in the face of life's worst.

The joy of salvation is anchored in the death and resurrection of Christ. His death belongs to this present evil age, and is, in fact, its most heinous crime.[54] His resurrection belongs to the age to come. It is the "first fruits" of a harvest that is still future.[55] In Christ the two ages have met, like two titans in combat, or, more accurately, like an invading force (the age to come) arriving to conquer an evil empire (this age). The enemy has not yet drawn his last breath, and in fact still seeks to wreak havoc wherever he can. In Luther's words, "His rage we can endure, for *lo, his doom is sure!*"[56] To be "in Christ," to use Paul's characteristic way of describing our status in redemption, is to live in one age, but to be a citizen of another. It is to live in evil's domain, but to belong to the rightful, conquering King. It is to suffer the gasping wrath of a dying regime, and at the same time be confident in our Champion's ultimate conquest. It is to be kept by his protective power, and to face the stiffest tests of life with the indomitable joy that only he can give.

Cosmic joy. Finally, as we think about the consummation of God's redemptive plan in the new heavens and the new earth, we must bring passages like these into our hope:

> Let the heavens be glad, and let the earth rejoice;
>> let the sea roar, and all that fills it;
>> let the field exult, and everything in it!
> Then shall all the trees of the wood sing for joy
>> before the LORD, for he comes . . . . (Psalm 96:11-12)

> Let the sea roar, and all that fills it;
>> the world and those who dwell in it!
> Let the floods clap their hands;
>> let the hills sing for joy together
>> before the LORD, for he comes . . . . (Psalm 98:7-8)

> For you shall go out in joy,
>> and be led forth in peace;
> the mountains and the hills before you
>> shall break forth into singing,
>> and all the trees of the field shall clap their hands . . . .
> (Isaiah 55:12)

Those of us who would feel at home in Lewis' Narnia or Tolkien's Middle Earth can imagine an animated nature rejoicing in its Maker. Is this how we are to take these passages? Will we behold this with the eyes of our glorified bodies in the new heavens and new earth? I hope so! But it is at least true that these cameos of redeemed nature are meant to tell us that a total environment of joy is the ideal for all created life, and that one day this will be realized.[57]

Martin Luther wrote that in the resurrection people will "play with heaven and earth, the sun and all the creatures." And "All creatures shall have their fun, love and joy and shall laugh with thee and thou with them . . . ."[58] When the ancient harmony of Eden is restored, and raised to even greater heights, all creatures – in ways suited to their creaturehood – will reflect the glory of the Creator, and will, in that mirrored glory, know the creature's share in the shared joy of the Father, Son and Holy Spirit. A flaming fire. A river of pleasure.[59]

QUESTIONS FOR THOUGHT AND DISCUSSION

1. How does our culture deny or diminish the seriousness of sin? Why is it important for us to come to grips with the bad news about our human condition before we can appreciate the good news of what God has done for us in Christ?

2. "Those who choose another god multiply their sorrows." (Psalm 16:4) How has this played out in your own life? The lives of people you know? Our culture? What are the gods of this generation?

3. Why is God's joy in our salvation important? Why is it important to see "joy regained" as the centerpiece of redemption? What difference does it make? What difference does it make to the way you talk with unbelieving friends about the Gospel?

4. Why is it important to link our present joy to the future joy of the Kingdom? What difference does this make to your experiences of joy?

5. How do you see the paradox of already-not-yet in your life and your experience? Why is it important to affirm both sides of the paradox? What implications are there if we only affirm one or the other?

CHAPTER 5

JOY AND THE WORD OF GOD

"Oh! How great and glorious a thing it is to have before one the Word of God! With that we may at all times feel joyous and secure."[1] Martin Luther wrote the words, but many have known this joy. Long before Luther, sacred poets reveled in the same pleasure:

> In the way of your testimonies I delight
>   as much as in all riches. (Psalm 119:14)

> I find my delight in your commandments,
>   which I love. (Psalm 119:47)

> Oh how I love your law!
>   It is my meditation all the day. (Psalm 119:97)

> How sweet are your words to my taste,
>   sweeter than honey to my mouth! (Psalm 119:103)

> Your testimonies are my heritage forever,
>   for they are the joy of my heart.[2] (Psalm 119:111)

Delighting in God's written Word to us is a high peak in the mountain range of joy. As we explore it we will begin on a broad path at its base, and then wind our way upward, narrowing our course as we approach its spectacular summit.

JOY AND OUR VISION OF LIFE

If you are like many, you separate the rational and emotional dimensions of our human nature. Theologians sometimes distinguish between "faculties" of the soul, such as intellect, emotion, and will.[3] Maybe you aren't that theoretical. Still, you may think that reason and emotions belong in different categories. They aren't the same kind of thing. Emotions seem like reflexes: they happen to us in an involuntary sort of way. Reason, on the other hand, is deliberate and intentional. Emotions are a spontaneous, and reason a studied, way of interacting with the world.

Actually, emotions are more complex than they seem when we experience them. They are rooted in our thought life. This is so because emotions are interpretive in nature. We don't delight in things unless we *perceive* them as something to be desired. We don't fear things unless we *regard* them as something that could be dangerous to us. We don't become angry with someone unless we *construe* their actions to be contrary to our expectations or desires. We don't grieve the loss of someone or something unless we *see* ourselves bereft of something we value.[4] Without this interpretive dimension (an activity of our minds) we would not have emotions as we know them. Robert Roberts puts it this way: "Human life, even when it is far from intellectual, is fundamentally a life of the mind."[5] In every emotion there is an act of interpretation, even if it happens so quickly and unobtrusively that we are unaware of it.

Let's see where this path takes us. Our interpretations of life never hang mid-air. They don't take place in isolation, ad hoc, or on their own. They are part of a larger web of beliefs we have about the world and our place in it. This is another way of talking about a worldview. A worldview is the lens through which we see the world and our life in it. It is the orientation of our hearts that gives us our bearings as we journey through life. It is the larger narrative framework in which we understand our story. Although we can and should think about our worldview, and think and reason from it, more often than not it operates tacitly, beneath the surface of our awareness. In the experience of an emotion we may not notice it at all. Nevertheless, it is always there, helping us make sense of life.[6] Worldviews are essential to emotions as we experience them.[7] Whether you've ever given a thought to it or not, you have one and it is crucial to your prospects for joy.[8]

Paul Holmer wrote: "Christian beliefs are like the river-bed for one's thoughts and emotions, within which contentment, peace and joy can truly flourish."[9] If you turn to the pages of Scripture, you will discover the same truth:

> Not only that, but we *rejoice* in our sufferings, *knowing that* suffering produces character . . . . (Romans 5:3)

> You *joyfully* accepted the plundering of your property, *since you knew* that you yourselves had a better possession and an abiding one. (Hebrews 10:34)

> *Count it all joy*, my brothers, when you meet trials of various kinds, *for you know* that the testing of your faith produces steadfastness. (James 1:2-3)

The sacred authors share a belief that joy flourishes in a vision of life in which our hearts are shaped and informed by the knowledge of God and his ways.[10]

JOY AND ITS REASONS

Josef Pieper wrote, "Man can (and wants to) rejoice only when there is a reason for joy. And this reason, therefore, is primary, the joy itself secondary."[11] We enjoy God *because* we believe that he is our Creator and Redeemer. We enjoy the world *because* we believe it to be the amazing work of our amazing God. We rejoice in our circumstances *because* we see them as the work of a sovereign Lord for our good. We rejoice in our salvation *because* we regard it as the highest and best gift that could ever be given to us in our plight. These are the reasons for joy. Take them away, or prove them false, and joy would disappear with them.[12]

Where do we learn the truths that are essential to joy? Where do we learn the reasons for joy? From God, as he has made himself known to us through prophetic voices, supremely through his Son, our Lord Jesus Christ, and through the witness of the apostles – all vouchsafed to us in the Sacred Scriptures.[13] The path to joy leads us here:

> Long ago, at many times and in many ways, God spoke to our fathers by the prophets, but in these last days he has spoken to us by his Son, whom he appointed the heir of all things, through whom also he created the world. (Hebrews 1:1)

> For whatever was written in former days was written for our instruction, that through endurance and through the encouragement of the Scriptures we might have hope. (Romans 15:4)

> You have known the Holy Scriptures, which are able to make you wise for salvation through faith in Christ Jesus. All Scripture is God-breathed and is useful for teaching, rebuking, correcting and training in righteousness, so that the servant of God may be thoroughly equipped for every good work. (2 Timothy 3:15-16, NIV)

"Man shall not live by bread alone, but by every word that comes from the mouth of God." (Matthew 4:4)

Paul wrote to the church in Rome: "May the God of hope fill you with all joy and peace *in believing*."[14] Joy is God's gift to those who believe, to those who affirm that his Word to us is true.[15] This is not optional for joy. It is the only environment in which joy can flourish and grow. The Scriptures give us the truths that are essential for joy. They give us the reasons for joy, which we embrace in a life of faith. (Declining biblical literacy among those who profess faith in Christ, and the loss of joy in our generation, are linked, ball and chain. A Bible on the shelf is powerless to bring joy!)

JOY AND THE DISCOVERY OF TRUTH

Have you ever wondered why the discovery of truth is exhilarating?[16] Why did Archimedes jump from his bathtub and run naked into the street, crying "Eureka!" when he realized how to prove that the king's golden crown was a fraud? Why do we respond with an "Aha!" when the moment of discovery comes, instead of meeting it with a yawn? Why is there an irrepressible impulse to tell others? Why is it nearly impossible – whatever the field of knowledge – to keep the news to oneself? Because there is delight in discovery. Truth unveiled occasions joy as beauty evokes aesthetic pleasure, and a good joke brings laughter. Why is this so? Why do we find joy in the discovery of truth? This is how Augustine would have answered the question: "For a happy life is joy in the truth. For this is joy in You, who are the truth."[17] Underline the other side of this colon: Our joy in discovering truth is always, and never less than, a connection with the God of all truth.[18]

Whether we know it or not, it is the encounter with God in every discovery of truth that brings joy. C.S. Lewis pictured truth as a shaft of divine glory striking our minds.[19] To change the metaphor, all truth wafts the fragrance of its Homeland. Joy is our pleasure in its heavenly bouquet. We do not create truth. We can only discover it.[20] It is given to us. It is revealed. Disclosed. However it comes to us, whatever its mode of reception, all truth is from God. It is the encounter with him that brings us joy.

If all truth is God's truth, we may enjoy it wherever it is discovered.[21] Augustine wrote: "All good and true Christians should understand that truth, wherever they may find it, belongs to their Lord."[22] Calvin had the same vision of life:

> Not a particle of light, or wisdom, or justice, or power, or rectitude, or genuine truth, will anywhere be found, which does not flow from him, and which he is not the cause; in this way we must learn to expect and ask all things from him, and thankfully ascribe to him whatever we receive.[23]

> In reading profane authors, the admirable light of truth displayed in them should remind us, that the human mind, however much fallen and perverted from its original integrity, is still adorned and invested with admirable gifts from its Creator. If we reflect that the Spirit of God is the only fountain of truth, we will be careful, as we would avoid offering insult to him, not to reject or condemn truth wherever it appears. In despising the gifts, we insult the Giver.[24]

Enjoying his gifts glorifies the Giver.

To discover truth in nature is to touch the garment of God. To find it in our humanity is to see his reflection. To learn it in history is to trace the fingers of his sovereign hand. To encounter truth in Scripture, however, is to hear his beckoning voice and behold the beauty of his countenance. Here is one of our greatest joys! Calvin was right:

Now this power which is peculiar to Scripture is clear from the fact that of human writings, however artfully polished, there is none capable of affecting us at all comparably. Read Demosthenes or Cicero; read Plato, Aristotle, and others of that tribe. They will, I admit, allure you, delight you, move you, enrapture you in wonderful measure. But betake yourself from them to this sacred reading. Then, in spite of yourself, so deeply will it affect you, so penetrate your heart, so fix itself in your very marrow, that compared with its deep impression, such vigor as the orators and philosophers have will nearly vanish. Consequently, it is easy to see that the Sacred Scriptures, which so far surpass all gifts and graces of human endeavor, breathe something divine."[25]

This is what we mean when we call the Bible the "inspired Word of God." It is God-breathed.[26] It is the product of his creative breath. It breathes truth *from* God *about* God and his ways. There is no truth nobler than this. No truth loftier or more sublime. And so it is that there is no joy-in-truth greater than joy in God's Word.

JOY AND THE GOD OF THE WORD

Joy in the Word of God is always at the same time joy in the God of the Word. This is so because biblical revelation, by its very nature, is both personal and propositional.[27] The inspired Word is both a coming of God and communication from God. It conveys the presence of God and truth about God and his ways. It is both event and word, relational and intelligible, self-disclosing and informative.

It is important for us to speak of both dimensions of biblical revelation because the written Word is the Word of the living God. The Spirit who inspired the Word continues to speak through the Word. What he once communicated through the pen of sacred scribes he speaks today through the same written Word. Stephen spoke of "living oracles" given to future generations through Moses.[28] Peter wrote of the "living and abiding word of God."[29] And the writer of Hebrews added:

> For the word of God is living and active, sharper than any two-edged sword, piercing to the division of soul and of spirit, of joints and of marrow, and discerning the thoughts and intentions of the heart. And no creature is hidden from his sight, but all are naked and exposed to the eyes of him to whom we must give account. (Hebrews 4:12-13)

The Bible is the living Word of the living God. In it the breath of God is dynamically present. In Calvin's words again, "the Sacred Scriptures, which so far surpass all gifts and graces of human endeavor, breathe something divine." In his conversion from atheism, Emille Cailliet, former professor of Princeton Theological Seminary, discovered that the pages of the Bible are "animated by the Presence of the Living God and the Power of His mighty acts."[30] In the entire world there is no other literature like this!

We wander from the path if we separate the Word of God and the Spirit of God in our understanding of the Bible. In the words of Donald Bloesch, "The word that proceeds from the mouth of God is filled with the power of the Spirit, bringing life and renewal to those dead in sin. . . . The Word derives its efficacy from the Spirit and the Spirit teaches what he has already disclosed in the word of Scripture." [31] The practical import of this union of the Word and the Spirit is that joy in God's Word is always at the same time joy in the God of the Word. It is joy in the truth given in Scripture, and joy in the Truth-giver whose presence is known and whose voice is heard in the written Word.[32]

THE JOYS OF MEDITATION

Joy can come to us through reading the Scriptures, or hearing them recited, preached, or sung. It comes most powerfully, because it engages our inner life most fully, in meditation. When we reflect deeply on the Word of God, the joys that we have explored in this chapter converge in a single point.[33]

Joy and our vision of life. Let's retrace some of our steps. Joy, like all emotions, is interpretive in nature. It is perspectival. It flourishes and is most robust in a God-centered vision of life that is formed and informed by his Word. Now, how does this become ours in a way that results in joy? What takes the Word of God into the deep currents of our hearts where our understanding of life is formed and our way of living is shaped? What sinks the Word into our innermost being where God delights to see truth at work?[34] Meditation.

To understand why this is so, we can use Jonathan Edwards' distinction between two kinds of knowing: "There is a distinction to be made between a mere *notional understanding*, wherein the mind only beholds things in the exercise of a speculative faculty; and *the sense of the heart*, wherein the mind not only speculates and beholds, but *relishes* and *feels*."[35]

A cursory reading of the Bible yields a *notional understanding* of what is written. An understanding of words and ideas. Some people never get beyond this in their knowledge of the Scriptures. It is in meditation, in the sacred interface between the Spirit-inspired Word and a Spirit-filled heart, when the lines between reflection, worship, and prayer become blurred and even insignificant, that the deep affections of our hearts are engaged and transformed by truth. It is this *sense of the heart* – the aim of meditation - that creates the conditions for joy.

A *notional understanding* of God and his ways will change nothing about us. A *sense of the heart* can change everything. In sensing and savoring truth – the heart of meditation – we are transformed by it.   It touches our formative values: the things we treasure and hold dear at the most profound level of who we are. It changes our interests and concerns, our hopes and fears, our dreams and aspirations. It transforms what we think about and how we think about it.[36] It forges new ways of understanding the world, and creates a new vision of life.

Joy and the discovery of truth. Meditation embraces a paradox: Truth is both disclosed and discovered. It is revealed, but we must open ourselves to the revelation. It comes to us, but we must pursue it. And we must pursue it with passion:

> Yes, if you cry out for insight
> and raise your voice for understanding;
> if you seek it like silver
> and search for it as for hidden treasures;
> then you will understand the fear of the LORD
> and find the knowledge of God.
> For the LORD gives wisdom;
> from his mouth come knowledge and understanding.
> (Proverbs 2:3-6, RSV)

Meditation does not create a Zen-like void within. It creates a heart filled with thoughts of God. It is not cool, detached reflection. It is white hot, ablaze with a desire to know God and his ways. It is involved, invested, intent, and even intense. It is never mere observation. It is more like an obsession!

These are the essential features of meditation: disclosure, discovery, and delight. God discloses truth to us; we discover what he has disclosed; when disclosure and discovery meet, we experience great delight. Hearts devoted to God and his Word enjoy truth not as information but as illumination. Not merely as proposition, but as pleasure. God's Word becomes honey to our hearts, and a feast to our souls:

How sweet are your words to my taste, sweeter than honey to my mouth! (Psalm 119:103)

Your words were found, and I ate them, and your words became to me a joy and the delight of my heart (Jeremiah 15:16).

Joy and the God of the Word. I promised you a majestic summit when we began our climb. Here it is: The joy of meditation reaches its peak in the enjoyment of God who speaks through his Word. This joy begins with the cry of our hearts, "Beyond the sacred page, we seek thee, Lord!"[37] It is fulfilled as the sacred Presence is mediated through the sacred Page. It is not just a knowing, but a meeting. An encounter. At its highest and best, meditation is reflecting on the Word of God in the presence of God. As one Old Testament scholar put it, "The heart of meditation is the sheer enjoyment of the presence of the living Lord."[38] It is seeking communion with God in his Word, as the Spirit who once inspired the Word now creates a spiritual fellowship through the Word. If you have experienced this joy, accepting anything less would be like running a race but stopping short of the finish line, like ending a climb at a lower peak when the summit and its breathtaking vistas are within reach, like settling for an appetizer when the entrée is still to come:

> My soul is feasted as with a rich feast,
>   and my mouth praises you with joyful lips,
> when I think of you on my bed,
>   and meditate on you in the watches of the night. (Psalm 63:5-6, NRSV)

The enjoyment of God in his Word is a consummate pleasure, as the truth of God illumines our minds, the will of God captivates our wills, the splash of his presence refreshes our hearts, the sound of his voice beckons us, and the beauty of his perfections holds us spellbound. Nothing will center your life, focus your heart, strengthen your resolve, assure you of truth, and encourage you in a God-pleasing life more than an encounter with the Living Lord through the Living Word.

QUESTIONS FOR THOUGHT AND DISCUSSION

1. What difference does it make to understand that your emotional life and your thought life are interrelated?

2. What difference is there between these two statements, and how would you respond to someone who affirms the second, but not the first?

   "All truth is God's truth."
   "Everything is true."

3. What implications are there for seeing all truth as a connection with the God of truth?

4. How does it help you to make a distinction between a "notional understanding" and a "sense of the heart" in the way you approach the Scriptures? How have these two kinds of knowledge played out in your Christian life?

5. Describe your experience with meditation. How does it compare with the discussion of meditation in this chapter? Have you been inspired or encouraged to make changes? If so, in what ways?

CHAPTER 6

ENCOUNTERING GOD IN HIS WORD

W e should give thanks for the men and women whose scholarship helps us understand the Bible, and take advantage of their work if we can. We should also be thankful, however, that we don't need to be scholars to read the Bible in ways that bring us into an encounter with God and a heart-shaping, thought-directing, life-changing, relationship with him.[1] An open Bible and an open heart are all that is necessary for joy.

LECTIO DIVINA

As you study the Scriptures, let me recommend an ancient practice to you: *lectio divina*.[2] It is a way of interacting with the Word of God for the sake of communing with God.[3] It includes four movements of the heart: *lectio* (reading), *meditatio* (meditating), *oratio* (praying) and *contemplatio* (contemplating).[4]

Lectio. In the ancient world not many could read, and even fewer possessed copies of the Scriptures. For most people the reading of the Word was an auditory event: listening to someone read to them. Jewish people gathered in synagogues to hear the Scriptures read. Early Christians did the same when they assembled and their leaders fulfilled the apostolic injunction: "Devote yourself to the public reading of Scripture."[5]

Let this shape your *lectio*, or reading of the Scriptures. Think of reading as listening. Picture yourself in the synagogue in Nazareth, listening to Jesus read the Sacred Word to you:

> And he came to Nazareth, where he had been brought up. And as was his custom, he went to the synagogue on the Sabbath day, and he stood up to read. And the scroll of the prophet Isaiah was given to him. He unrolled the scroll and found the place where it was written,
>
>> "The Spirit of the Lord is upon me,
>>   because he has anointed me
>>   to proclaim good news to the poor.
>> He has sent me to proclaim liberty to the captives
>>   and recovering of sight to the blind,
>>   to set at liberty those who are oppressed,
>>   to proclaim the year of the Lord's favor."
>
> And he rolled up the scroll and gave it back to the attendant and sat down. And the eyes of all in the synagogue were fixed on him. And he began to say to them, "Today this Scripture has been fulfilled in your hearing." And all spoke well of him and marveled at the gracious words that were coming from his mouth. (Luke 4:16-22)

Or imagine yourself in this setting with Jesus and two disciples after the resurrection:

> That very day two of them were going to a village named Emmaus, about seven miles from Jerusalem, and they were talking with each other about all these things that had happened. While they were

talking and discussing together, Jesus himself drew near and went with them. . . . And he said to them, "O foolish ones, and slow of heart to believe all that the prophets have spoken! Was it not necessary that the Christ should suffer these things and enter into his glory?" And beginning with Moses and all the Prophets, he interpreted to them in all the Scriptures the things concerning himself. (Luke 24:13-27)

In the discipline of *lectio* we read, eager to be addressed. We read, longing to hear the word of Christ. We read, picturing Christ himself reading to us, opening the Scriptures to us. We read, listening with rapt attention to him.

The reading involved in *lectio* should not only engage your mind, but your imagination and your affections. Bring yourself wholly to the Sacred Word, and allow it to address every dimension of who you are. Just as God spoke in "many and various ways" to our ancient family of faith,[6] so he does to us today.[7] He may address your mind with truth that illumines the path of life. His Word to you may strike your imagination with vivid pictures that enable you to *see* truth for your life. He may speak to your hopes and fears, your longing for love, your cry for peace, your yearning for significance, your desire for joy. *Lectio* seeks and is open to all of this.

As you read the Scriptures in a daily regimen for spiritual health, take note of passages and verses that capture your attention, and come back to them in your *lectio*. Read your chosen text at least twice. Many recommend reading aloud. The first time through, read without stopping. Then read it again slowly, attentively, and expectantly, with your mind alert and your heart open to possibilities: "Read the text selected at least once aloud, and then repeat it more slowly until you are stopped by a word or phrase that speaks to you. Listen for the word that seems to shimmer, beckon, unnerve, or challenge you. You are listening for God's voice in the sacred text."[8]

Meditatio. You are now ready for the second movement in *lectio divina*: Meditation. Reading the Scriptures whets your spiritual appetite; in meditation you eat your fill and enjoy. Reading the Word gives you a taste; in meditation you relish and delight. Reading gives you the lay of the land; in meditation you walk a path, linger along the way, stop, and sit for a while to appreciate and enjoy your surroundings.

When he was faced with temptation, Jesus quoted the ancient Scripture, "Man shall not live by bread alone, but by every word that proceeds from the mouth of God."[9] The Word of God is spiritual food. It feeds and nourishes us in our life with God. Sadly, we've become too accustomed to "fast food" and "eating on the run" to appreciate this metaphor. Meditation is a meal in which we sit, take our time, eat slowly, ruminate (literally, "chew"), and savor as we are filled.[10]

In your *meditatio*, focus on a word or phrase that arrested your attention in your reading. Stay here. There is only one Voice you want to hear. Put a finger to your lips and hush all others. Clear your mind of every distraction. Picture every diversion walking out of the room, leaving you quiet before God, in a position to give him your full attention. Be purposeful. Focus. Affirm God's presence with you.

Read the text again and again. Repetition is essential to meditation. Let it become a rhythm. Reflect on the sacred words and pay attention to the thoughts that come to you. Explore them. Let them lead you into new terrain. If images come to your mind, let them come clearly into view. How do they illumine what you've read? How do they relate to you and your life with God? Lower the guard you have set around your emotions, and open your heart to ways in which God may wish to speak to this important dimension of who you are. Let his Word bring sorrow, grief, conviction, joy, delight, hope, thankfulness, wonder, awe, or courage. Trust God with your vulnerability in this moment. Thank him for his loving, careful touch. Give freedom to your emotions and embrace them as part of God's communication with you. Be prepared to laugh or to weep!

Oratio.[11] Prayer isn't something we add to our reading and meditation. It is the Godward focus of all that we are doing. We approach our reading of the Scripture prayerfully, asking God to meet with us, to guide and direct us, to speak to us. We set aside any agenda that we may have, and come to the Scriptures with the prayer, "Not my will but yours be done."[12] As we move into meditation, prayer is an inner attentiveness. An openness and readiness to hear God's voice, and to see whatever he may show us. It is the invitation, "Speak, LORD, for your servant in listening."[13]

Oratio is also a distinct movement in *lectio divina*. Begin by incorporating your chosen text into a prayer. Let its words become yours, offered back to God. Personalize them with your own name. Rewrite them with "I" "me," "my." If they are *about* God, translate them into language addressed *to* God. If inspiration comes, sing them to God. He is your only audience, and he welcomes your musical offering! If the words of the text don't lend themselves to a prayer, hold the open Scriptures upward to God, and let the lifting up of your hands be your prayer.[14]

As you interact with a sacred text in meditation you will find yourself touched, stirred, and invited to respond. Whatever your response, wrap it in prayer and present it to God. It may be a prayer of longing and desire. It may be a prayer of worship and wonder. It may be a prayer of thanksgiving. Maybe it will be a prayer of confession and sorrow. You may find yourself striving with God, wrestling with challenges and questions in your life. You may be stirred to implore God to act in some way in your life or in the world around you. God may bring others to your mind and you will pray for them. It may be prayer without words, because you simply can't find them.[15] It may be a listening prayer as you wait before God to hear his voice. It may be a thankful recognition of God's presence with you.

Contemplatio. The word *contemplation* is a visual term.[16] It involves looking at something with steady focus and continued attention. We might contemplate the vastness of the universe, or the beauty and wonders of the world. It is a way of seeing things in a certain way as a result of careful and continuous observation. In our context, contemplation involves directing the "eyes of our hearts" to God,[17] and then envisioning the world through the Scriptures – which reveal God's vision of the world to us, filtered through the limitations of our humanity.[18]

Reading, meditating, and praying the Scriptures will bring a new perspective on life. We see God, the world, ourselves, and others in ways that we otherwise would not. We see things in light of who God is, what he has done, what he is doing, and what he has pledged to do. The apostle Paul wrote to the church in Corinth, "For the love of Christ controls us, because we have concluded this: that one has died for all, therefore all have died; and he died for all, that those who live might no longer live for themselves but for him who for their sake died and was raised."[19] Contemplate this long and clearly enough, and you will see yourself and others in a different way: "From now on, therefore, we regard no one according to the flesh. Even though we once regarded Christ according to the flesh, we regard him thus no longer. Therefore, if anyone is in Christ, he is a new creation. The old has passed away; behold, the new has come."[20]   This leads us to a second way in which we use the word "contemplation." It involves imagining possibilities in ways that lead us to act in ways that we otherwise would not. For instance, a young couple might contemplate marriage. They imagine what it would be like. They see themselves in that covenant relationship. They picture its potential. They envision its possibilities. Doing this results in decisions they make and a path they take. Or a couple might contemplate retirement from the work force. They imagine what life might look like if they were to take that action, they put themselves in imagined life scenarios, and then they make decisions and set a course for themselves as a result.

When the apostle Paul contemplated the love of Christ and his sacrificial death and resurrection, he saw people in a new and different way. This in turn led him to envision the world in a new light, to see new possibilities, to see himself in those possibilities, and to embrace a course of action to which God was calling him:

> All this is from God, who through Christ reconciled us to himself and gave us the ministry of reconciliation; that is, in Christ God was reconciling the world to himself, not counting their trespasses against them, and entrusting to us the message of reconciliation. Therefore, we are ambassadors for Christ, God making his appeal through us. We implore you on behalf of Christ, be reconciled to God. (2 Corinthians 5:18-20)

Contemplatio envisions bold new possibilities for our world and places us squarely in the mix. It brings a new awareness of the world as God sees it, and then activates and energizes us to participate with him in what he is doing. We become agents of redemption. In Christ, through us, God reconciles the world to himself. This is amazing. Truly amazing!

Make the disciplines of *lectio divina* a way of life. Make them a way of living in the Word and by the Word. There is formative power here that will change you. There is a fullness and fruitfulness in life that can only be found here. There is an intimacy with God that you can only enjoy here. There are pleasures of the heart that only those who walk this path can know:

In the way of your testimonies I delight
    as much as in all riches. (Psalm 119:14)

I find my delight in your commandments,
  which I love. (Psalm 119:47)

Oh how I love your law!
  It is my meditation all the day. (Psalm 119:97)

How sweet are your words to my taste,
  sweeter than honey to my mouth! (Psalm 119:103)

Your testimonies are my heritage forever,
  for they are the joy of my heart. (Psalm 119:111)

QUESTIONS FOR THOUGHT AND DISCUSSION

1. Spend time in the Scriptures every day for a week, using the interactive questions found in Endnote 2 of this chapter. How did this change your time in the Word? How did this play out in your life in ways that caught your attention?

2. How does reading-as-listening change your approach to the Scriptures? Is it helpful to imagine Christ reading the Word to you, and listening to him? If you did this, describe your experience.

3. After implementing the discussion of *meditatio* in this chapter, describe how it engaged your imagination and emotions in ways that were meaningful to you.

4. As you reflect on your practice of *lectio divina* in the last week, what part did prayer play? In what ways were you led to pray in response to your meditation?

5. As you practice *lectio divina*, how do you see your vision of life changing? How do you see yourself changing to become part of this new perspective? In what ways do you sense yourself being summoned to be part of what God is doing?

CHAPTER 7

JOY AND CIRCUMSTANCES MISUNDERSTANDINGS

L ife without circumstances would be like having another birthday without growing any older. As much as you might wish it were otherwise, you can't have one without the other. Life without circumstances is a mere abstraction. There is no such thing for us. Because this is so, some of the most important terrain we can explore is the relationship between joy and the circumstances of our lives. How does joy connect with the day-to-day scenarios that comprise so much of what we experience? Let's begin by looking at wrong answers to this question.

Wrong answer: Joy is unrelated to circumstances. Many Christians would say that this statement is true. Their reasoning goes something like this: God transcends our circumstances; our joy is in God; therefore joy transcends our circumstances.[1] They are not connected. If this sounds right, how can it be wrong?

Whether we like it or not, we must all live in a given time, in a particular place, under specific conditions. Joy must be circumstantial because life is circumstantial, and joy is meant for life. It isn't something that hovers above the plane of events as we experience them.   Joy is the rain of heaven,   but it falls upon the earth. It meets us in our natural and historical existence. It is related to the environment and events of our life, as they in turn are related to a good, wise, all-powerful, and ever-present God. (In other words, transcendence is not the only truth about God that is relevant for joy.)

Those who think that joy is unrelated to circumstances appeal to the apostle Paul: "Rejoice *in the Lord* always!"[2] You must choose between the Lord and circumstances, they say. If you choose the first, you get joy. If you choose the second, the best you get is happiness.[3]   It is worth noting, however, that in the same letter we see Paul talking about joy in the circumstances of his life. He rejoiced in the anticipation of being released from prison.[4] He hoped to be cheered by the coming of Timothy.[5] He rejoiced when his financial conditions were improved by a gift from the Philippian church.[6] The choice between the events of our life and the Lord of our life is false. Joy-unrelated-to-the-circumstances-of-life is as far removed from Paul's view (and his experience, from what I can tell) as anything could be. Look at his exhortation again: "Rejoice in the Lord *always*." His God-centered understanding of joy embraced life in all of its situations and scenarios.

What you are about to read is extremely important: *To say that joy is unrelated to circumstances etherealizes joy and encourages people to seek it elsewhere than in the life God has actually given them.* In seeking it somewhere else, they will not find it. (This is the only life we get in this world. There won't be another. Wake up to this, and do it before you waste another day – even another moment – wishing that God had given you something else!) Joy comes to us in and through the circumstances of life as they are ordered by a sovereign and loving heavenly Father who is always with us. Joy is not only related to circumstances, it is intended for us in all of them. That is a very different prospect.

Wrong answer: Joy is related only to favorable circumstances. This shares a kinship with Aristotle's understanding of happiness. Happiness, he taught, consists of "good birth, plenty of friends, good friends, wealth, good children, plenty of children, a happy old age, and also such bodily excellences as health, beauty, strength, large stature, athletic powers, together with fame, honour, good luck and virtue."[7] If happiness requires these things, the happy are few indeed! This is an elitist understanding of what it means to flourish in life. If these advantages are ours, it is entirely appropriate to find joy in them. For the Greeks they were the whims of fortune or fate. For the Christian they are gifts from a good God. If they are received with thankful hearts, and offered back to God in worship, our pleasure in them is transposed upward into the octaves of joy.

Joy is not limited to positive circumstances, however. Centuries before Aristotle, the prophet Habakkuk found joy bereft of the things the philosopher esteemed so highly:

> Though the fig tree do not blossom,
>   nor fruit be on the vines,
> the produce of the olive fail
>   and the fields yield no food,
> the flock be cut off from the fold
>   and there be no herd in the stalls,
> yet I will rejoice in the LORD,
>   I will joy in the God of my salvation. (Habakkuk 3:17-18, RSV)

Not only is joy possible in the absence of favorable circumstances, it can be ours when hardship comes our way. Pascal wrote, "I live with joy, whether in the prosperity which it pleases Him to bestow on me, or in the adversity which He sends for my good."[8] This was the hallmark of early Christianity, modeled and taught by Christ himself:

Blessed are you when others revile you and persecute you and utter all kinds of evil against you falsely on my account. Rejoice and be glad, for your reward is great in heaven. (Matthew 5:11-12)

Then they left the presence of the council, rejoicing that they were counted worthy to suffer dishonor for the name. (Acts 5:41)

I rejoice in my sufferings. (Colossians 1:24)

You had compassion on those in prison, and you joyfully accepted the plundering of your property, since you knew that you yourselves had a better possession and an abiding one. (Hebrews 10:34)

Count it all joy, my brethren, when you meet trials of various kinds. (James 1:2)

Rejoice insofar as you share Christ's sufferings. (1 Peter 4:13)

Aristotle was apparently a stranger to this experience. His philosophy may represent the pinnacle of pagan happiness; it is barely a foothill before the majestic mountains of joy.[9]

Wrong answer: Joy is oblivious to the harshness of life. If we were to give a name to this approach to joy, it would be *Pollyanna*. Pollyannaism refuses to come to grips with the trials and tribulations of life. It simply ignores them and insists that nothing is wrong with the world. It is willing to sacrifice realism for peace, and truth for serenity. This is not the path the Bible takes. It is relentlessly realistic. It meets the perils and pains of life head-on. William Temple wrote, "Christian joy and hope do not arise from an ignoring of the evil in the world, but from facing it at its worst."[10] Joy does not pretend that night is day; its radiant beams dispel the darkness and keep the shadows at bay. Joy does not turn its back on evil; it measures its boundaries and lays claim to its territory. It gives the devil his due and then robs him of his plunder.[11]

Ancient followers of Jesus discovered joy in the midst of trials because they saw them as spiritually significant.[12] They believed that their hearts would be shaped through them. They looked at the ordeals they went through and saw new possibilities for developing endurance, character, and hope.[13] They saw an opportunity to share in the holiness of God and to gain what they saw as "the peaceful fruit of righteousness."[14] They believed that the other side of their trial would bring them into a greater steadfastness, maturity, and completeness.[15] They were not masochists. They did not find joy *in* suffering, but *through* it. They most certainly did not ignore it.

Wrong answer: Joy comes to us despite adversity. This approach to joy is the polar opposite of Pollyannaism. It does not ignore the dangers and perils of life; it knows them all too well. They simply don't factor into its equation of joy. It says, in fact, that if joy is experienced in the course of trials, it is always in spite of them. It reads the Scriptures this way:

> Blessed are you *despite* the fact that men may revile you and
> persecute you and utter all kinds of evil against you on my account.
> Rejoice and be glad.

> Then they left the presence of the council, rejoicing, *in spite of the fact* that they had suffered for the name.

> I rejoice *despite* my sufferings.

> You were joyful *despite* the plundering of your property.

> Count it all joy, my brethren, *despite the fact that* you may meet various trials.

> Rejoice *in spite of the fact* that you share Christ's sufferings.

If you re-read these passages from an earlier paragraph in this chapter, you will see the problem. This isn't what the texts say! The difference in wording may seem small, but the difference in significance is enormous. This approach to life is counterproductive to joy. It is God's way to bring joy *in and through* difficult circumstances, not *in spite* of them.[16] To make joy contrary to the hardships of life destroys that process and forfeits the joy he intends. God transforms sorrow into joy, and brings joy through sorrow and even in the midst of sorrow. He does not give us joy in spite of our sorrows.[17]

Wrong answer: Joy is insulated from hardship. Some Christians approach joy this way. It isn't that they are unaware of the pain and difficulties of life. They shut their heart's door to them and retreat to a place where they hope to be cocooned in a calm and peaceful state. They seek a joy that is "serene and untouchable . . . independent of all the chances and changes of life."[18]

Think for a moment about what it would take for you to remain tranquil and untouched by life's dangers, perils, and trials. You could withdraw from the world and seek shelter from the storms of life. You might avoid some of life's dangers as a hermit, but many would still find you. Even if it were possible to exempt yourself from the troubles of life through retreat, it would not be true to the joy of Jesus (and so would always be a counterfeit). Paul Tournier was right: "Our attitude to life is always a reflection of our attitude to God. Saying "Yes" to God is saying "Yes" to life, to all its problems and difficulties – "Yes" instead of "No," an attitude of adventure instead of going on strike. In such an adventure we commit our entire being. It is not an escape."[19]

If we take the Incarnation seriously, our model for living in the world will not be one of withdrawal, but involvement. Costly involvement. In Jesus, God entered into, and fully engaged, the life we know. He embraced it, thorns and all. He drank its cup to the dregs. Indeed, it was in the thorns of his passion and the dregs of his suffering that his joy came into clearest focus.[20] Joy does not avoid the thorns of life; it fashions them into a crown. It does not run from life's dangers; it faces them with courage. It meets tribulation with "good cheer" because its source is the One who has overcome the world.[21]

Joy does not lie in withdrawal from the world and its perils. If you are willing to grant this, but still think that joy is being serenely untouched by life's trials, you will have to take a different path: not the course of physical withdrawal, but emotional denial. This was the way of the Stoics. You will have to train your heart in the disciplines of apathy, indifference, and detachment, so that you will be able to meet every event with cool equilibrium. William Barclay describes the Stoic way of life:

> (The Stoics) . . . proposed to eliminate all emotion until a man had come to a stage when he did not care what happened either to himself or to anyone else. Epictetus says. "Begin with a cup or a household utensil; if it breaks, say, 'I don't care.' Go on to a horse or a pet dog; if anything happens to it, say, 'I don't care.' Go on to yourself, and if you are hurt or injured in any way, say, 'I don't care.' If you go on long enough, and try hard enough, you will come to a stage when you can watch your nearest and dearest suffer and die, and say, 'I don't care.'" The Stoic aim was to abolish every feeling of the human heart."[22]

On the contrary, joy is not the repudiation of our emotions, but their consummation and crown. Denying the emotional dimension of our lives does not create room for joy, it lays waste to the only atmosphere in which joy can exist. Joy cannot flourish in an emotional vacuum, or in an emotional desert. It cannot thrive in an apathetic wasteland.

Joy transforms our response to the trials of life, but is not untouched by them. It changes our hearts; it does not make them impervious. The paradigm is found in Christ's words, "*Happy* are those who *mourn*: they shall be comforted,"[23] and is fleshed out in Paul's experience: "We are treated as impostors, and yet are true; as unknown, and yet well known; as dying, and behold, we live; as punished, and yet not killed; as sorrowful, yet always rejoicing."[24] You will remain a stranger to joy until you face difficulties with realism and embrace the fact that your emotions are meant to be an essential part of your response to life.

QUESTIONS FOR THOUGHT AND DISCUSSION

1. How did you understand the relationship between joy and the circumstances of your life before reading this chapter? Has this chapter changed your mind? If so, how?

2. What is the difference between Aristotle's understanding of happiness and the author's understanding of joy?

3. According to the author, how is joy different from a Stoic version of happiness?

4. Do you see "Pollyannaism" in popular understandings of joy and the circumstances of life? In your family? Your church? Among your friends? How is true joy different from this?

5. As a result of reading this chapter, what will you do differently about the way your respond to your circumstances?

CHAPTER 8

FINDING JOY IN THE CIRCUMSTANCES OF LIFE

CIRCUMSTANCES AND THE PRESENCE OF GOD

Now that we've examined wrong answers to the question of how joy is related to the circumstances of life, we are ready for the truth of the matter. We will need to craft a *theology of circumstances*. Let's start at the beginning. Our word "circumstance" comes from the Latin, *circum*, which means "around," and the verb, *stare*, which means "to stand." Circumstances are the conditions that "stand around" us and affect our lives. They are factors of time, place, and events that shape much of what we experience.

Our biggest challenge in discovering joy in our circumstances is that we don't see our circumstances related to God. For centuries Christians believed that while God is never to be identified with his creation (because he is transcendent), he nevertheless fills it (because he is also immanent). He is everywhere present within the universe. He inhabits all space, but is confined to none. If this is true, then he is present in all of our circumstances. The Bible teaches us to think this way:

> Yet he is not far from each one of us, for "in him we live and move and have our being." (Acts 17:28, RSV)

Do I not fill heaven and earth? declares the LORD.
(Jeremiah 23:24)

Where shall I go from your Spirit?
   Or where shall I flee from your presence?
If I ascend to heaven, you are there!
   If I make my bed in Sheol, you are there!
If I take the wings of the morning
   and dwell in the uttermost parts of the sea,
even there your hand shall lead me,
   and your right hand shall hold me. (Psalm 139:7-10)

As 21st century followers of Jesus we may try to believe this, but the culture in which we live makes it difficult to be convinced of it in practice. The Spirit of the Age encourages us to see our circumstances without God in the picture, to believe that if there is a God, he is unrelated and indifferent to the conditions in which we live. Even if we live in a postmodern world, we are heirs of the Enlightenment. We live among devotees of "scientism."[1] We are influenced by the social dynamics of secularization. All of this has the effect of banishing God from the world in the minds of many. It is in the air we breathe. It is a film over our eyes, clouding our spiritual vision. It is oil to the water of joy in the circumstances of our lives.

There is only one solution to this problem: the renewing of our minds. "Do not conform to the pattern of this world, but be transformed by the renewing of your mind."[2] This does not make God present to us. It positions us to discern his presence. It tunes our thoughts and aligns our affections in ways that increase our awareness of his company. The renewing of our minds is not mere information, but a robust reformation: a restructuring of our inner life that takes place as the Spirit of God makes the Word of God alive and active in our hearts.[3] It is the renovation of our thoughts and a reshaping of our affections so that we see life differently and treasure what we see. As we give ourselves to this process we discover joy in the truth that God is the chief Circumstance in all our circumstances. He is the nearer Presence in all that is present to us.[4]

We should not think of the omnipresence of God as if he were stretched out to fill every nook and cranny in the universe. Nor is his ubiquity merely "his freedom to be in space," or the fact that "everything is included in his overall vision."[5] The truth is that we don't know how Spirit relates to space.[6] If we engage in speculation, we will understate or overstate, and surely misstate, the case. I can't tell you how the divine Presence is related to the space we inhabit, but I believe that God is nevertheless really present. I believe, further, that you will remain at a shouting distance to joy in difficult circumstances until you embrace this for yourself.

When the Psalmist wrote, "They draw near who persecute me with evil purpose . . . but you are near, O LORD,"[7] the latter Circumstance was as real to him as the former – and far more significant. The sons of Korah experienced God as a "very present help in trouble."[8] David knew the company of his Lord even as he walked through the "valley of the shadow of death."[9] Sacred poets described the presence of God as a refuge, a fortress, and a shield as they faced the challenges of life.[10] For generations, people of faith have found strength these reassuring words:

> Fear not, for I have redeemed you;
>   I have called you by name; you are mine.
> When you pass through the waters, I will be with you;
>   and through the rivers, they shall not overwhelm you;
> when you walk through fire you shall not be burned,
>   and the flame shall not consume you . . .
> Fear not, for I am with you. (Isaiah 43:1-5)

God is present in our lives in every moment, at every turn, and in every situation. It is who God is and what he does. There is no escaping his presence,[11] but we can ignore it. We can be out of touch with it. We can miss it.

Or not.

We can practice the presence of God.[12] We can live in fellowship with him. We can listen for his voice, seek his face, and celebrate his presence with thanksgiving and praise. We can keep the Lord always before us. Always at our right hand.[13] Always in our "mind's eye."[14] Like a radio that has been tuned to receive unseen sound waves that surround us at all times, our hearts can be tuned to God's company and the music of his presence in all that comes our way.

CIRCUMSTANCES AND THE PROVIDENCE OF GOD

God is not only present in our circumstances, he is present as Sovereign Lord. All things are his servants.[15] Willingly or not, everything in the universe – from quarks to mammoth stars, from a baby's yawn to the executive order of a president – bows to his purposes. This is where joy parts company with pagan views of happiness that treat circumstances in a fortuitous way. The very word *happiness* reveals that orientation to the events of life. Its root lies in the Danish word, *happe*, which means to happen by luck or by chance. To be happy in this vision of life is to have good luck, good chance, or good *hap*. Its "iffy" nature can be seen in the words per*haps*, *hap*hazard, and mis*hap*. It is contingent, uncertain, accidental. There is no plan or purpose of which it is a part. We see this in Shakespeare's *The Two Gentlemen from Verona*, when Proteus says:

> Wilt thou be gone? Sweet Valentine, adieu.
> Think on thy Proteus, when thou *haply* seest
> Some rare noteworthy object in thy travel.
> Wish me partaker in thy *happiness*
> When thou dost meet good *hap*; and in thy danger,
> If ever danger do environ thee.[16]

Joy could not exist in a chance universe. It is sustained by pattern and purpose. Its bread is the presence of God in all circumstances; its drink, his providential work in and through them. Joy is rooted in the deep truth: "To those who love God, who are called according to his plan, everything that happens fits into a pattern for good." [17] Our hearts do not rejoice in pleasurable circumstances merely because of their pleasure, but because they are part of the Pattern: God's sovereign commitment to our good. We can rejoice in difficult circumstances because they, too, are part of the Pattern: God's sovereign commitment to our good. The Pattern includes everything in its scope. Absolutely everything. Nothing is beyond its boundaries. Nothing whatsoever. This is why it is possible to find joy in every circumstance.

To view the world through a wide-angled lens, think of God as the sustaining Ground of all events in the universe (including events in your life). Every event, whatever its finite cause, is grounded in the Power that upholds all things. Nothing has power in itself. Nothing happens by itself. All things live and move and have their being in God. [18] He energizes all things. [19] Finite causes direct energy in finite ways — some of them sinful — but it is always borrowed energy, so to speak. It is sourced in the all-pervasive, sustaining power of God. [20]

God is not only the Ground of all things; he is their Governor. He knows and foreknows. [21] He guides and directs. He bends and shapes. He permits, but never merely permits. He intends and superintends. He rules and overrules. For some this immediately raises the issue of divine sovereignty and human freedom. How are they related? A fair question, but not one that I will pursue here. It is enough to say that human acts are both free [22] and teleological. [23] They are freely chosen, and at the same time serve the ends that God has designed and the plans he established before the foundations of the world. [24] I can't explain the relationship between God's will and human wills any more than I know how Spirit relates to space. I embrace the mystery. With the Psalmist I say, "I do not occupy myself with things too great and too marvelous for me."[25] It is the upholding power of God that makes all events possible, and his sovereign power that ensures their place in the Pattern.[26]

The Heidelberg Catechism defines the Providence of God thus:

> Providence is
>   the almighty and ever present power of
> God
>   by which he upholds, as with his hand,
>   heaven
>   and earth
>   and all creatures,
>   and so rules them that
>   leaf and blade,
>   rain and drought,
>   fruitful and lean years,
>   food and drink,
>   health and sickness,
>   prosperity and poverty --
>   all things, in fact, come to us
>   not by chance
>   but from his fatherly hand.[27]

"All things, in fact, come to us not by chance but from his fatherly hand." This is what makes joy possible in any event and every circumstance. The power of God lies beneath all that happens, sustaining it, and over every event, governing it. Everything happens for the good of those who love God and are called according to his purpose. Ultimately, all things serve the glory of God. This is the Pattern. Even if we grasp a very small part of its grandeur, this is where our hearts find joy.

JOY AND THE SIGNIFICANCE OF CIRCUMSTANCES

Significance is to joy what food is to the body. First century followers of Jesus saw this clearly:

> More than that, we *rejoice* in our sufferings, *knowing that* suffering produces character. (Romans 5:3)

> You *joyfully* accepted the plundering of your property, *since you knew* that you yourselves had a better possession and an abiding one. (Hebrews 10:34.)

> *Count it all joy,* my brethren, when you meet various trials, *for you know* that the testing of your faith produces steadfastness. (James 1:1-2)

We would not experience joy in our circumstances if we could not discern their import in part. It is in knowing the Pattern, seeing God's hand in our circumstances and his purposes in them, that we find joy. Silently and invisibly God is present in all that surrounds us and takes place in our lives. His sovereign hand is at work. It is the hand of a Craftsman, building spiritual qualities into our lives.[28] It is the hand of a Sculptor, molding us into the likeness of Christ.[29] It is in knowing that we live in the presence of God, that our lives are governed by the purposes of God, that our hearts are being shaped by the hand of God, that we are positioned for joy in all of life's scenarios.

JOY AND THE TRIUMPH OF CHRIST

Joy does not lie in submission to the challenging circumstances of life, but in triumph over them. The victory may be bloody: "We are afflicted in every way, but not crushed; perplexed, but not driven to despair; persecuted but not forsaken, struck down, but not destroyed."[30] It is victory nonetheless:

"But thanks be to God, who in Christ always leads us in triumph."[31] It may seem to others that we have been vanquished, but they cannot see the flag of conquest flying in our hearts: "We are treated as impostors, and yet are true; as unknown, and yet well known; as dying, and behold, we live; as punished, and yet not killed; as sorrowful, yet always rejoicing; as poor, yet making many rich; as having nothing, yet possessing everything."[32]

The triumphant joy of the Christian in the midst of difficulty is a share of Christ's victory over the powers arrayed against God: "In the world you have tribulation; but be of good cheer, I have overcome the world."[33] It is a foretaste of our ultimate victory over mortality through the resurrection of Christ:

> Behold! I tell you a mystery. We shall not all sleep, but we shall all be changed, in a moment, in the twinkling of an eye, at the last trumpet. For the trumpet will sound, and the dead will be raised imperishable, and we shall be changed. For this perishable body must put on the imperishable, and this mortal body must put on immortality. When the perishable puts on the imperishable, and the mortal puts on immortality, then shall come to pass the saying that is written:
>
> "Death is swallowed up in victory."
> "O death, where is your victory?
>   O death, where is your sting?"
>
> Thanks be to God, who gives us the victory through our Lord Jesus Christ. (1 Corinthians 15:51-57)

Knowing that the bonds of God's love in Christ can never be broken, joy fears nothing in the universe:

Who shall separate us from the love of Christ? Shall tribulation, or distress, or persecution, or famine, or nakedness, or danger, or sword? . . . No, in all these things we are more than conquerors through him who loved us. For I am sure that neither death nor life, nor angels nor rulers, nor things present nor things to come, nor powers, nor height nor depth, nor anything else in all creation, will be able to separate us from the love of God in Christ Jesus our Lord. (Romans 8:35-39)

To borrow a term from J.R.R. Tolkien, joy sees our calamities as *eucatastrophes*. They are "good catastrophes." God brings a small good from them in the present as a preview of the far greater good that he will bring at the end of time.[34] Our joy now is but a brief glimpse of the far greater Joy that awaits us. Tolkien used this as a literary motif in his stories, but it is a reflection of the real-life tale believers know as they discover joy in the midst of their trials:

The eucatastrophic tale is the true form of fairy-tale, and its highest function . . . . It does not deny the existence of *dyscatastrophe*, of sorrow and failure: the possibility of these is necessary to the joy of deliverance; it denies . . . universal final defeat and in so far is *evangelium*, giving a fleeting glimpse of Joy, Joy beyond the walls of the world, poignant as grief . . . . In such stories . . . we get a piercing glimpse of joy, and heart's desire, that for a moment passes outside the frame, rends indeed the very web of story, and lets a gleam come through.[35]

Joy in the midst of life's circumstances, even in our trials, is the joy of the Kingdom, which has penetrated the present in advance of its final consummation.[36] It rends indeed the very web of *history*, and lets a gleam come through. It is a foretaste of the new heavens and the new earth. An installment. The first fruits of the joy in God's undimmed presence and the pleasures forevermore held in his hand.[37] Joy is the closest thing to heaven that we will experience on our fallen planet. It is closest because it is a bit of heaven itself. It is a brand from heaven's fire. A spark from heaven's blazing glory. A breath of heaven's air. A fragrance from its orchards. A bar of its music. A beam of its light cast onto this dark world.

Joy points us to a better world, but not at the expense of this one. It does not remove us from this world; it strengthens us to live within it. It doesn't make us blind to this world's troubles; it gives us the courage to face them. Like a soldier's pocketed photo of his beloved in the heat of battle, joy not only reminds us of our true home, it gives us something worth fighting for, and courage to fight on. Joy does not counsel us to surrender to life's trials; it emboldens us to conquer in the name of Christ, assured that even if we should lose the hour, we will win the day. Even if we should lose a battle, in Christ, and with him, we will win the war.

DRAWING NEAR TO GOD IN OUR CIRCUMSTANCES

Near to God we find joy. There are three kinds of nearness in this regard.[38] The first is the nearness of measurable space. If two things are close to each other in this way, the distance between them is small. The smaller the space, the nearer they are. Because God is everywhere present, he is always near in this way. The apostle Paul told his audience in Athens that God is never far from us, since "in him we live and move and have our being."[39] God is above, below, behind, before, to the right, and to the left of all things. He not only surrounds us, he is within us. He is as near to us as the breath in our lungs, the blood in our veins, the thoughts in our minds, and the affections of our hearts. In Augustine's words: "You [are] more intimately present to me than my innermost being."[40] We can never be nearer to God in our circumstances than we already are. It is something we affirm and for which we give thanks.

It should be often in our thoughts, and often in our praise and worship of God.

Spatial nearness is one thing; relational nearness is another. Two people seated next to each other on a crowded city bus may be close to each other in the first sense (measurable space) but far from each other in this second way (relational proximity). They may not know each other at all. When we talk about "close friends," this is the nearness we have in mind. It is possible to near or far from God in this way:

> The LORD says: 'These people come near to me with their mouth and honor me with their lips, but their hearts are far from me. (Isaiah 29:13)[41]

> The LORD is near to the brokenhearted. (Psalm 34:18)

> The haughty he knows from afar. (Psalm 138:6)

This nearness to God is a nearness of hearts. It is a relational closeness that grows from common values, interests, and concerns. Shared affections. Shared life. It is a personal and even an intimate relationship with God. This is what the Psalmist had in mind when he wrote, "I am continually with you; you hold my right hand."[42] And "But for me it is good to be near God."[43]

How do we experience this nearness of God in our circumstances? It isn't at our command at a moment's notice. It is a cultivated way of life. A congeniality of hearts. It is a nearness to God that is nurtured as our hearts are aligned with his. When he is often in our thoughts and treasured in our affections. When our wills beat in rhythm with his. When we love what he loves and hate what he hates. When we view our circumstances through the lens of his Word to us. When we ask in every situation, "Lord, what are you doing, and how can I join you?"

Finally, there is the nearness of similitude or likeness. If a painter seeks to capture a vase of flowers on a canvas and succeeds in doing so, we say that the painting is "close" to the original. It is like the original. We were created in the image of God, and that likeness is restored in us as the Spirit of God shapes our hearts so that we become like Christ.[44] His virtue becomes ours. The more like Christ we are, the closer to him we will be. Because it is grounded in who we are, we can enjoy this nearness in all the situations and circumstances of life.

QUESTIONS FOR THOUGHT AND DISCUSSION

1. "To those who love God, who are called according to his plan, everything that happens fits into a pattern for good." (Romans 8:28) How is joy related to this truth?

2. Do you see God as the nearer Circumstance in all your circumstances? What obstacles in your vision of life stand in the way of embracing the presence of God in every situation you are in?

3. Why is it important to affirm both the transcendence of God over your circumstances, and his presence with you in them?

4. If you have read J.R.R. Tolkien's *Ring Trilogy*, or seen the movies, how do you see his concept of "eucatastrophe" play out in the plot? How have you seen this in your life?

5. How would you characterize the "nearness of relationship" and the "nearness of approximation" in your relationship with God and what is important to you? How do you see this impacting the prospects for joy in your circumstances?

Chapter 9

MARRIAGE: EDEN'S JOY

I f there is an institution endangered in our day, it is marriage and family. Though it would be worth exploring, I will leave how this factors into the demise of our culture to others. My concern here is the loss of joy that inevitably attends the weakening and destruction of these relationships. Tear the fabric, destroy the joy in its delicate weave. My interest is revisiting ancient insights into marriage and family as a foundation for human flourishing, and persuading as many as possible that there is great joy to be found here!

There is no better place to begin our exploration than the teaching of Jesus. When he was asked to give his views on marriage, his starting point was not later chapters in the human narrative that show this relationship in its fallenness and sin, but the very first chapter of our story, where we see God's intention and design unmarred by our failings. This is what he said:

> Have you not read that he who created them *from the beginning* made them male and female, and said, 'Therefore a man shall leave his father and his mother and hold fast to his wife, and the two shall become one flesh'? So they are no longer two but one flesh.

What therefore God has joined together, let not man separate. (Matthew 19:4-6)

Because of your hardness of heart Moses allowed you to divorce your wives, but *from the beginning* it was not so. (Matthew 19:8)

At his word, we will begin with the opening lines of the human story.

MARRIAGE AND THE IMAGE OF GOD

When was the last time you attended a wedding ceremony that celebrated marriage as a display of God's image in humanity? Not sure you can think of any? Yet that is what this relationship is meant to be:

Then God said, "Let us make mankind in our image, in our likeness, so that they may rule over the fish in the sea and the birds in the sky, over the livestock and all the wild animals, and over all the creatures that move along the ground."

So God created mankind in his own image,
    in the image of God he created them;
    male and female he created them. (Genesis 1:26-27, NIV)

To say that God is a Trinity is to affirm, even if we will never fully fathom, that he is a community of Persons – Father, Son, and Holy Spirit – who share a bond of love with each other and eternally delight in the beatitude of their shared love. To say that we were created in the image of this God – which is the first thing we learn about ourselves in the sacred Scriptures – is to say that we were made to mirror God in finite, embodied ways in the world he created. It is not our design, but the Creator's. Our understanding of marriage should begin here.

In the opening chapter of the human story we discover that Adam-alone was not Adam-complete. Following a series of benedictions, "And God saw that it was *good*,"[1] we find this exception: "Then the LORD God said, 'It is *not good* that the man should be alone.'"[2] Why? Because we were made to live in community. We are fulfilled and find our identity in life shared with others. While humans-as-such bear the image of God ("In the image of God he created them."), it is in relationships, and especially in our gendered relationships as men and women and as husbands and wives, that we bear the image of God together ("Male and female he created them.").[3] This is fundamental to our humanity, and essential to the good and wise intentions of our Creator. It is foundational to God's plan for marriage.[4]

The story develops:

> Then the LORD God said, "It is not good that the man should be alone; I will make him a helper fit for him." Now out of the ground the LORD God had formed every beast of the field and every bird of the heavens and brought them to the man to see what he would call them. And whatever the man called every living creature, that was its name. The man gave names to all livestock and to the birds of the heavens and to every beast of the field. But for Adam there was not found a helper fit for him. So the LORD God caused a deep sleep to fall upon the man, and while he slept took one of his ribs and closed up the place with flesh. And the rib that the LORD God had taken from the man he made into a woman and brought her to the man. Then the man said,
>
> > "This at last is bone of my bones
> > and flesh of my flesh;
> >   she shall be called Woman,
> > because she was taken out of Man." (Genesis 2:18-23)

In the inspired narrative of our beginnings Adam was in the Garden with the animals he named. As he watched creatures in gendered pairs, he knew that someone was missing from his life. One day he awoke from a deep sleep to discover that the Creator had brought another to him – like him,[5] and yet different from him in ways that caught the breath in his throat, quickened the beat of his heart, rushed the blood through his veins, and stirred new and powerful emotions and desires within him. When he beheld this new creation in her unclothed feminine splendor, the exclamation of astonished delight leapt from his lips: "This at last is bone of my bones and flesh of my flesh!"

From that moment on, Eden held pristine possibilities for the first couple, fully envisioned by the Creator and yet to be discovered by them. In body and soul they would share an intimacy of life, love, and joy that mirrored the life, love, and joy of the Triune God who made them.

TWO BECOME ONE

There is an infinite chasm between God and everything else. He is incomparable. *Sui generis.* Yet his Word also tells us that he created humans in his image. There is an analogy between God and us, designed and disclosed by the Creator himself.[6] This not only enables us to think and talk meaningfully about God, it helps us understand who we are and the task he has given to us as his image-bearers. This illumines the creation story, retold in the words of Jesus:

> [Jesus] answered, "Have you not read that he who created them from the beginning made them male and female, and said, 'Therefore a man shall leave his father and his mother and hold fast to his wife, and the two shall become one flesh'? So they are no longer two but one flesh. What therefore God has joined together, let not man separate." (Matthew 19:4-6)

Although he might have chosen another way, in his creative wisdom the Triune God crafted a finite, embodied reflection of his oneness in the unity ("one flesh") and life-long commitment ("What therefore God has joined together, let not man separate.") of a man and woman ("he . . . made them male and female").[7] Together-as-one-for-a-lifetime.[8] The union of husband and wife in the covenant of marriage is a sign that points to a higher, greater, spiritual reality. Their gendered unity offers a faint glimpse of the eternal union of the Triune God in human experience.[9]

Like their Triune Maker, Adam and Eve formed a communion of equals. Equal in their participation in the image of God, and evenly matched in the dignity of that status. Their bond of mutual love and shared joy would not have been possible otherwise. Adam didn't need a lesser being to share life with. He needed someone who, with him, would bear the image of God. He needed someone whom he could describe with the words "bone of my bone and flesh of my flesh." Neither one greater, neither lesser.[10]

Like the Persons of the Trinity, Adam and Eve were equal and yet wonderfully different. Their oneness did not negate their differences, but made them complementary, each enhancing and enriching the other, together singing in harmony, dancing in step across the Garden floor. The contours and capacities of their bodies were a perfect fit. Their nuanced masculine and feminine gifts created possibilities together that neither had apart from the other. Only Adam could pleasure Eve and contribute to the wonder of fruitfulness that made her "the mother of all living."[11] Only Eve could pleasure Adam and through their shared delight make him a father of children and the representative of all mankind.[12] As they ventured into life together, only Adam could husband Eve.[13] Only Eve could help Adam.[14] Their pleasure lay in delighting in their differences, and through them, becoming one. One in life. One for a lifetime. Masculine and feminine in a joyful embrace, fulfilling the call to bear God's image in the world.

Naked and Unashamed

In their union Adam and Eve *knew* each other.[15] This is not a euphemism for people who feel uncomfortable talking about sex. It is a positive description of intimacy and transparency, disclosure and discovery, between a man and woman in which they give themselves fully to each other. "And the man and his wife were both naked and were not ashamed."[16]

In the Garden Adam and Eve would not have known what privacy was or why one would want or need it. If you had told them that nudity in their relationship should be veiled, you would have seen confusion in their eyes and heard loud guffaws of incredulity in response. There was nothing to hide. There were no secrets. There was no vulnerability. No need to protect oneself from the other. In time Adam and Eve in the Garden would have come to know as much as they could about each other, and would have delighted in every detail.

Adam was welcomed and embraced by Eve as God's gift to her. He entrusted himself fully to her. Eve was genuinely impressed with Adam's manliness, and knew that this pleased him greatly. There were only words of admiration and generous approval, spoken truly from her heart, in praise of his masculine form. He was handsome and strong in her eyes, and that was the only mirror he had. That is how he saw himself. There was no need to be brash, because he knew that he was fully desirable to his wife as he was. There was no need to hide what made him so obviously different from Eve. Modesty had no meaning and served no purpose. He enjoyed pleasing Eve with his body, delighting in the knowledge that giving himself fully to her enriched and fulfilled her sexuality in the Creator's good and wise design.[17]

Eve was welcomed and embraced by Adam as God's gift to him. She entrusted herself fully to him. There were only words of appreciation and affirmation, spoken truly from his heart, in praise of her feminine form. She was beautiful in his eyes, and that was the only mirror she had. That is how she saw herself. There was no need to flaunt her features, because she knew that she was fully desirable to her husband as she was. There was no need to be demure. Modesty had no meaning and served no purpose. She enjoyed pleasing Adam with her body, delighting in the knowledge that giving herself fully to him enriched and fulfilled his sexuality in the Creator's good and wise design.[18]

FRUITFULNESS

In their innocence Adam and Eve were neither takers nor misers. Each was a generous giver and an enjoyable gift. They delighted in giving and receiving pleasure, loving and being loved, knowing that this reflected something of the love and joy of their Creator. Their masculine and feminine bodies enabled them to express their love to each other in ways that were unique to each and a pleasure to both. They experienced sexual pleasure as the beatitude of their shared love, and couldn't have imagined it any other way. This was the heart of the fruitfulness God had in store for them.

"And God blessed them. And God said to them, 'Be fruitful and multiply and fill the earth.'"[19] In these ancient words some see a moral obligation for married couples, if possible, to have children. Roman Catholics see procreation as a dictate of natural law. (If we let nature take its course in sexual relations, children are usually the result. It is nature's law, and therefore the Maker's law.) Protestants have often seen this text as a command to be obeyed.

Let me propose, instead, that these words are a blessing that results in the gift of children. Commands are to be obeyed; blessings are to be treasured and enjoyed.[20] Procreation is not a duty; children are not an obligation. It is all an expression of God's favor to enable us to flourish in life. It is meant for our joy. It makes a difference. A big difference![21]

If you find yourself unfamiliar or even uncomfortable with this, let me give you three reasons for considering it. First, why would Adam and Eve need a command to have sex (the only way to be fruitful and multiply)? I never had to command my children to eat their favorite food or play their favorite game. Second, if being sexually fruitful and having children is a moral imperative given to humans-as-such, then Jesus failed.[22] Really? Third, these very words were used of the animal kingdom earlier in the same chapter: "And God blessed them, saying, "Be fruitful and multiply and fill the waters in the seas, and let birds multiply on the earth."[23] Do fish and birds have the capacity to fulfill moral obligations? I don't think so, but the language is the same.

No, something else is happening here. This is the language of blessing. (How could we miss this when the words "Be fruitful and multiply" are prefaced with the words "And God blessed them"?) In the ancient Scriptures God blesses people, animals, land, dwelling places, crops and other things.[24] His blessing is an endowment of power. When God speaks in blessing, his word brings about the intentions of his heart. His blessings not only display his great might, they bestow his favor, and reflect his goodness and generosity toward his creatures.[25] This puts us in a better position to understand the text in Genesis 1. The marriage relationship is a blessing from God.[26] Sexual pleasure shared by a husband and wife is his blessing.[27] God created us in a way that we would, in fact, pursue this.[28] The mystery and wonder of conception, and the unseen growth of new human life in a mother's womb, are further blessings from our Creator. Children are a bonus from his good hand. They exhibit God's creative power and are meant for our joy.[29]

The primal blessing of marital fruitfulness plays two roles in fulfilling God's plan for our planet. It is integral to Creation and Redemption. Through the bearing and rearing of children we are enabled to fulfill the mandate to harness and steward the resources of the earth, and to marshal our God-given creativity for his glory and our good.[30] It is also through marriage and the gift of children, generation after generation, that God would one day bring his Son into the world as an infant, who would grow to be a man, to bring redemption to it.[31]

ORIGINAL JOY

Theologians have much to say about what they call *original sin*. It refers not only to the sin of our first parents, but the solidarity of the human race in that sin. It is crucial to our understanding not only of the human condition *in Adam*, but to our understanding of redemption, and the status of the redeemed *in Christ*.

Too little attention is given to *original joy*.[32] For a time it bound all of creation together. It was the nexus of our relationships with each other and with God, and a mirror of God's Triune joy on the earth.[33] Marriage is meant for our joy. Family life is meant to multiply it, filling the earth with children who will become husbands, wives, and parents, creating an ever-expanding joy in our Maker and a shared joy in all that he has made. Do you not long for this? Does it not beckon you?

QUESTIONS FOR THOUGHT AND DISCUSSION

1. How does this chapter's discussion of the image of God help you understand the Trinity? And how does this understanding of the Trinity influence your view of marriage?

2. "And the man and his wife were both naked and were not ashamed." What does this imply about their relationship? What kind of relationship would have to be the case for this to be true?

3. How does the phrase "equal and yet wonderfully different and complementary" illumine the Trinity and your understanding of male and female in a marriage relationship? How does this differ from other relational models that are advocated in our society or in the Church?

4. Do you see the words, "Be fruitful and multiply" as a command to be obeyed? What difference would it make to see this not as command, but a blessing? How might this impact the problems of unwanted or undervalued children in our society?

5. Have you seen Eden in marriages you know of? What impresses you about these couples? What do you see in them that you want for yourself?

Chapter 10

Marriage
Far as the Curse is Found

The Fall has taken a terrible toll on our kind. Ripples from the primal stone thrown into the pond of humanity have reached shore all the way around. We may think that our fallen condition is normal because we are used to living with it, but it is far, far from that. Marriage and family, the most foundational and formative relationships we have, are mutant. Misshapen. Dysfunctional. It is our own doing, and now it is our undoing.

The garment of marriage and family is in tatters. We have witnessed the unraveling of its seams in our day. Many see marriage as a dispensable (or at least pliable) convention. Fewer marry. Many wait longer to marry. Half who marry, divorce. Many go to great lengths to limit childbearing. Couples who could have children choose not to. Parents pay others to care for their children while they seek to fulfill personal aspirations.

Sex has been ripped from its sacred origins, stripped of its essential meaning, and torn from the context of marriage. We have sown the wind are reaping a whirlwind![1] The land is now strewn with casual sexual liaisons, prolific pornography, sexual perversion and violence, domestic abandonment and abuse, abortion, and sanctioned infanticide.² Broken marriages, broken families, and broken people lie in the wreckage.

The tale of tragedy began here:

> The LORD God took the man and put him in the garden of Eden to work it and keep it. And the LORD God commanded the man, saying, "You may surely eat of every tree of the garden, but of the tree of the knowledge of good and evil you shall not eat, for in the day that you eat of it you shall surely die."

> The woman . . . took of its fruit and ate, and she also gave some to her husband who was with her, and he ate. Then the eyes of both were opened, and they knew that they were naked, and they sewed fig leaves together and made themselves loincloths.

> To the woman [the LORD God] said,

> "I will surely multiply your pain in childbearing;
>   in pain you shall bring forth children.
> Your desire shall be for your husband,
>   and she shall rule over you."

> And to Adam he said,

> "Because you have listened to the voice of your wife
>   and have eaten of the tree
> of which I commanded you,
>   'You shall not eat of it,'
> cursed is the ground because of you;
>   in pain you shall eat of it all the days of your life;
> thorns and thistles it shall bring forth for you;
>   and you shall eat the plants of the field.
> By the sweat of your face you shall eat bread,

till you return to the ground,
for out of it you were taken;
for you are dust, and to dust you will return.
(Genesis 2:15-17; 3:6-8, 16-19)

The world changed that day. It pivoted and moved in a different and dire direction. Adam and Eve hid from God and then from each other. Sin brought guilt. Guilt brought shame. Shame became the mirror in which they saw themselves. Intimacy and harmony gave way to distance and dissonance. Memories of their pristine love and joy grew dimmer by the day. Affirmation and affection were lost to criticism and blame. The delicate balance of gendered equality and difference became a tug-of-war and sometimes all-out-war, between the sexes. The joys of sexual love gave way to the perverted pleasures of lust. Sibling rivalry and murder followed in the wake.

Woe to us! Eden was such a short chapter in our story; the Fall so lurid and long. The image of God, once our treasured status and the centerpiece of marriage, shuffles like a beggar in dirty rags through trashed alleys of our own making.

NO MORE LET SIN OR SORROWS GROW!

Imagine the damage of the Fall undone! If you know the Christmas carol *Joy to the World,* feel free to sing this verse:

No more let sin nor sorrows grow,
nor thorns infest the ground.
He comes to make his blessings flow
far as the curse is found.[3]

Many Christians are quick to affirm God's grace as a preparation for heaven, but are not as swift to see the possibilities of grace on the earth in the present. Yet this is where the Curse is found. This is exactly where God intends to see his blessings flow. This is where he purposes to change factors in the human equation that sum to sorrow's rule.[4]

Starting with Jesus. In the last chapter we saw that when Jesus taught about marriage he refused to take his cues from this relationship in its fallen state, or even from the Scriptures that accommodate our hardness of heart. His standard was nothing less than God's original design in creation. *For Jesus, the beginning is still binding.* Eden is still God's intention and desire for men and women who enter marriage. Let's read these words again:

> Have you not read that he who created them *from the beginning* made them male and female, and said, 'Therefore a man shall leave his father and his mother and hold fast to his wife, and the two shall become one flesh'? So they are no longer two but one flesh. What therefore God has joined together, let not man separate. (Matthew 19:4-6)

> Because of your hardness of heart Moses allowed you to divorce your wives, but *from the beginning* it was not so. (Matthew 19:8)

I understand that following Jesus in pursuit of Eden makes me vulnerable to the charge of impossible idealism. I won't concede the point. If Jesus had been a shrewd politician he would have stepped back from his controversial statement in order to appease opponents and gain supporters.[5] He wasn't; he didn't; nor will I. Because I have fallen short of God's design doesn't mean that I shouldn't pursue it or point others to it. If I fail, it doesn't mean that you should not make the attempt.[6]

The disciples of Jesus responded to his teaching on marriage and its high standards with the despairing comment that it would surely be better not to marry.[7] Jesus knew the high divorce rate in first century Jewish culture.[8] He knew that Moses had permitted divorce.[9] But he also knew that there is an importance difference between *accommodation* and *aspiration*: God's *accommodation* to our sinful condition and his *aspiration* for us. If they had understood him, his disciples would have responded, "If the hardness of our hearts keeps us from God's desire for our lives, may they become soft and malleable in his hands!" The quality of your marriage and family life begins here. What will become of them, what is possible or impossible for them, starts here.

Understanding ideals. Part of our problem may be a misunderstanding. An ideal is impossible only if we think of it as all or nothing. If it is, our hands will be forever empty. But that isn't the nature of ideals. They are optimal qualities. They represent life at its best. We don't arrive at them; we move toward them. We stay on the path that leads us to them, or wander from it and lose sight of them. Ideals make demands of us, like intentionality, the formation of habits, customs, and long-term commitments; they do not, however, demand perfection in the pursuit. If we understand God's design for marriage as an ideal for us to pursue, we can see how it is possible to say "Yes" to Jesus and follow him, even if more of the path lies before us than behind.

Innocence and the possibilities of grace. We must make a distinction between these two things. The ship of innocence sailed long ago and left us behind. But God hasn't! His grace offered and given to us through Christ creates possibilities that would otherwise be entirely beyond our reach. It can re-create God's original design for marriages and families. It can restore the hearts of husbands and wives, parents and children, and brothers and sisters. Grace can do what we would bet our life savings against if it were up to us, because it is the loving action of the One who is with us, in us, and has all power at his beck and call.

In the same chapter of Matthew's Gospel in which Jesus taught God's ideal for marriage (and received a skeptical response), he pointed to the peril of riches and our need to release them from our grip (and again met with a skeptical response). His words apply to both: "With man this is impossible, but with God all things are possible."[10] Do you believe this? If you don't, you will walk a path of certain disappointment. If you do, the path will open onto vistas you cannot yet see that will take your breath away![11]

Marriage as a reflection. What was given in Creation and lost in the Fall God intends to restore in Redemption. All that was meant for our kind in Eden God intends to make possible for us wherever we make our home. At its heart, this is about the image of God and our calling to reflect the Creator in our lives. As grace renews the image of God in us, smudges and distortions are removed from the reflection. Integrity and wholeness are restored. Health begins and grows. As we are transformed, our life-long commitment to each other in marriage mirrors the eternal union of the Trinity. Our love for each other – the bond of marriage – pictures the bond of love between the Father, Son and Holy Spirit.[12] Our growing joy in each other reflects the overflowing joy of our Triune God.

The primal calling in marriage is still our primary calling. There is more to marriage than this, but not less. There is more to this relationship than meets the eye, but what can be seen is meant to direct attention to the God who made us in ways that honor him. Our understanding of marriage must begin here.

Marriage as a sacred covenant. Our culture sees marriage as a social contract, with terms, conditions, provisions, and rights. If this is what marriage is, any contract will do. Just fill in the blanks with the names of the consenting parties and let them negotiate the stipulations. The disagreement in our day is whether the participants must be male and female, or may also be the same gender.[13]

In a Christian vision of life, marriage in its intended and most robust sense is not a civil union but *holy matrimony*. A sacred covenant. It is sacred not only because of its divine origin and purpose,[14] and its blessing by Christ,[15] but because its members are three: a man, a woman, and Christ. Its covenant is a pledge of faithful love between a husband, a wife, and the Lord of their marriage.

Marriage is meant to mirror Christ and his relationship with the Church. In the words of the apostle Paul:

> Be filled with the Spirit, addressing one another in psalms and hymns and spiritual songs, singing and making melody to the Lord with your heart, giving thanks always and for everything to God the Father in the name of our Lord Jesus Christ, *submitting to one another out of reverence for Christ.* (Ephesians 5:18-21)

> *Wives, submit to your own husbands, as to the Lord.* For the husband is the head of the wife even as Christ is the head of the church, his body, and is himself its Savior. Now as the church submits to Christ, so also wives should submit in everything to their husbands. (Ephesians 5:22-24)

> *Husbands, love your wives, as Christ loved the church and gave himself up for her,* that he might sanctify her by the washing of water with the word, so that he might present the church to himself in splendor, without spot or wrinkle or any such thing, that she might be holy and without blemish. (Ephesians 5:25-27)

Christ is not a third party in the sacred covenant of marriage, but the first. He does not join us. We join him. He is not an addition to marriage. He is first in rank and relationship. Husbands see Christ first, in reverence honor him, then see and honor their wives through him. Wives see Christ first, in reverence honor him, then see and honor their husbands through him.   This is not mere symbolism. It is meant to shape all facets of married life. Everything is to be included; nothing left out.

In a beautifully nuanced mutual submission,[16] a husband is called to give himself in preferential love to his wife, and a wife is called to give herself in deferential love to her husband.[17] Lover and beloved bow before each other. Each honors the other. Each seeks the good of the other and does this joyfully: "singing and making melody to the Lord." Each offers a self-giving love, and seeks to out-give the other. Neither does this with merit in view; both do this from their reverence for Christ.

The bond of the marriage covenant is not merely between a husband and a wife, but between lover, beloved, and the One who loves them both, loved them first, and loves them best. There is great joy in seeing your marriage mirror the love relationship between Christ and his Church. Jonathan Edwards wrote:

> The mutual joy of Christ and his church is like that of bridegroom and bride, in that they rejoice in each other, as those whom they have chosen above others, for their nearest, most intimate, and everlasting friends and companions.
>
> Christ and his church, like the bridegroom and bride, rejoice in each other, as those that are the objects of each other's most tender and ardent love. . . . [Christ] loved the church, and gave himself for it; and his love to her proved stronger than death. And on the other hand, she loves him with a supreme affection; nothing stands in competition with him in her heart: she loves him with all her heart. Her whole soul is offered up to him in the flame of love.
>
> Christ and his church rejoice in each other's beauty.
>
> Christ and his church, as the bridegroom and bride, rejoice in each other's love.

Christ and his church rejoice in communion with each other, as in being united in their happiness, and having fellowship and a joint participation in each other's good: as the bridegroom and bride rejoice together at the wedding-feast, and as thenceforward they are joint partakers of each other's comforts and joys. [18]

Marriage and sacrament. A sacrament is a sign of the sacred among us. It points beyond itself to a transcendent reality. Baptism and the Lord's Supper are two examples.[19] A sacrament points us to Christ in our midst. When marriage is a sacred covenant between a husband, a wife, and their Lord, it becomes sacramental. It is a token of the gracious presence of Christ: "'Therefore a man shall leave his father and mother and hold fast to his wife, and the two shall become one flesh.' This *mystery* is profound, and I am saying that it refers to Christ and the church."[20] (Ephesians 5:32)

When this truth is embraced and lived, there is nothing ordinary about marriage. Everything a couple does in their relationship can celebrate the presence of Christ and point others to him. Their shared joy becomes a dance that others watch and want to join.

QUESTIONS FOR THOUGHT AND DISCUSSION

1. Discuss the breakdown of marriage and family as you see it in our day. Even in their fallenness, how can marriage and family contribute to human health and wellbeing?

2. Read Matthew 19:4-10, and then this quote from the chapter: Jesus' "standard was nothing less than God's original design in creation. *For Jesus, the beginning is still binding.* Eden is still God's intention and desire for men and women who enter marriage." How is Jesus' view of marriage different from what you see in our culture and often in the Church?

3. How does an understanding of ideals help your approach marriage and family life?

4. What is the difference between marriage as a sacred covenant and a social contract? What difference does it make?

5. What do you think of the discussion of the nuanced mutual submission of husbands and wives under Christ? Is it true to the Scriptures? Is it true to what you know about Christ?

CHAPTER 11

MARRIAGE AND FAMILY
EDEN AND MORE

Marriage and family as vocation. When you see the word "vocation," work probably comes first to your mind. In a Christian vision of life, however, vocation is much more than this. It encompasses every dimension of life, including marriage and family. After giving instructions on marriage and singleness to the church in Corinth, the apostle Paul wrote: "Only, as the Lord has assigned to each one, as God has *called* each, in this manner let him walk. And so I direct in all the churches."[1] Marriage and family are not only institutions ordained by God; they are callings.[2] Vocations. A married man is not a husband because he was declared to be so in a wedding ceremony. He is called by God to be a husband. A married woman is not a wife because she agreed to be so on the day of her wedding. She is called by God to be a wife. Children aren't children simply because they were born to a mother and a father. They are called by God to be children.

Martin Luther wrote:

> Likewise, those who are fathers or mothers, who rule their households well and who beget children for the service of God are also in a truly holy estate, doing a holy work, and members of a holy order. In the same way when children . . . are obedient to their

parents . . . this also is true holiness and those living in such estate are true saints on earth.[3]

It looks like a great thing when a monk renounces everything and goes into a cloister, carries on a life of asceticism, fasts, watches, prays, etc. . . . On the other hand, it looks like a small thing when a maid cooks and cleans and does other housework. But because God's command is there, even such a small work must be praised as a service to God far surpassing the holiness and asceticism of all monks and nuns. . . . there God's command is fulfilled, that one should honour father and mother and help in the care of the home.[4]

God has given this walk of life, fatherhood and motherhood, a special position of honor, higher than that of any other walk of life under it. Not only has he commanded us to love parents but to honor them. In regard to brothers, sisters, and neighbors in general he commands nothing higher than that we love them. But he distinguishes father and mother above all other persons on earth, and places them next to himself. For it is a much higher thing to honor than to love. Honor includes not only love, but also deference, humility, and modesty directed (so to speak) toward a majesty concealed within them. Honor requires us not only to address them affectionately and with high esteem, but above all to show by our actions, both of heart and body, that we respect them very highly and that next to God we give them the very highest place. For anyone whom we are wholeheartedly to honor, we must truly regard as high and great.[5]

If we could listen to the heart-talk of family members who understand the true nature of their relationships, this is what we would hear as they rise for a new day: "I am called this day to be a husband to my wife." "I am called this day to be a wife to my husband." "Lord, give us strength today to fulfill our calling as parents." "Help me fulfill the charge you have given me to honor my mother and father, and to love my brother and sister." We would see a prayerful purpose to fulfill these vocations in the events and tasks of the day.

Husbands are called to give themselves to their wives in sacrificial love and preferential care.[6] Wives are called to give themselves to their husbands in loving respect and deferential care. Together, parents are called to play a prophetic role in the lives of their children, speaking the Word of God into their lives; a priestly role in praying for their children and representing God to them; a protective role, sheltering them as they can from the dangers of the world; and a provisioning role, whether it is daily nurture, or the material goods that are necessary for life. There is great joy in fulfilling these callings from God!

Hallowed be this house![7] Marriage and family relationships are sacred. They are holy. Read with care these words from the apostle Paul:

> To the rest I say (I, not the Lord) that if any brother has a wife who is an unbeliever, and she consents to live with him, he should not divorce her. If any woman has a husband who is an unbeliever, and he consents to live with her, she should not divorce him. For the unbelieving husband is *made holy* because of his wife, and the unbelieving wife is *made holy* because of her husband. Otherwise your children would be unclean, but as it is, *they are holy*. (1 Corinthians 7:12-14)[8]

One Christ-follower in a marriage and family hallows these relationships. The presence of Christ in one makes a difference for all. Our Lord can accomplish much with little! Wherever there is faith in Christ, marriages and families are made holy, set apart by the presence of God and set apart for the purposes of God. This doesn't make them perfect or sinless (so there is no need to pretend that they are). God declares them holy on the basis of faith in Christ, and acts through them to bring about his purposes for the world.

The apostle Paul wrote to Timothy that marriage is good because it is the gift of a good God. He went on to say: "For everything created by God is good, and nothing is to be rejected if it is received with thanksgiving" by those who "believe and know the truth," for it is "*made holy* by the word of God and prayer."[9] God is holy. Temples are holy. Sacraments are holy. Angels are holy. We are accustomed to these associations. But marriage and family life? Not these relationships in the abstract, but in real life, everyday life, under the same roof? Meals at a table? Children at play? Cleaning the house? Mowing the lawn? This is God's Word, not mine: As his Word shapes our life together, and our prayers consecrate these relationships to his purposes, they are hallowed. All that they involve in day-to-day, feet-on-the-ground life becomes holy. They are set apart from the world and its sinful ways, and set apart for God and his purposes for the world.

Deo Gloria. For what are marriage and family set apart? They exist for the glory of God. It isn't that they do and other dimensions of life don't. All of life is meant for the glory of God, including marriage and family. Luther wrote of marriage:

> [God] wishes us to honor, maintain, and cherish it as a divine and blessed walk of life. He has established it before all others as the first of all institutions, and he created man and woman differently (as is evident) not for indecency but to be true to each other, to be fruitful, to beget children, and to nurture and bring them up to the glory of God. God has therefore blessed this walk of life most richly, above all others, and, in addition, has supplied and endowed it with everything in the world in order that this walk of life might be richly provided for. Married life is no matter for jest or idle curiosity, but it is a glorious institution and an object of God's serious concern.[10]

To affirm this for your marriage and your family is to embrace something truly wonderful: In these relationships you are caught up in something far greater than the little group that bears a family name, and shares life beneath the same roof. The "something greater" is God himself, his purposes for this world, and his honor in it. Your relationships exist to mirror truths about God and his ways. They are meant to point others to him.

Everything created by God can serve his glory. This includes marriage and family life in its day-to-day activities. It has been said of Luther: "[His] faith was simple enough to trust that after a conscientious day's labor, a Christian father could come home and eat his sausage, play his flute, sing with his children, and make love to his wife — all to the glory of God!"[11] If we are unfamiliar and uncomfortable with this robust vision of life made holy by God and devoted to his glory, it signals how far we have wandered from very important truths, how narrow our vision and how blinkered our spiritual eyes have become, and how lamentable we have made ourselves as a result. God wants so much more for us! The One for whom all things are possible can make this possible for your marriage, your family, your life.

COMMON GRACE FOR THE COMMON GOOD

The darkness of our world is pierced by shafts of light. The darkness is ours; the light is God's. He refuses to turn from us in our sin and shame, relentlessly pursues us, and seeks to woo us back to him and the joy of his redemptive love. In his mercy, God spares us the full impact of our rebellion against him. More than we know, he shields us from the growing and deepening evil in the world.[12] There are restraints within us (conscience) and around us (authority) for our protection.[13] In his grace God gives good things to remind us that he still would see us flourish under his hand. He gives many blessings and provisions to support and enrich our existence – not least of which are people providentially placed in our lives to nurture and care for us. Husbands and wives. Mothers and fathers. Sisters and brothers. Aunts, uncles, and cousins. Grandparents. God intends them for our good.

In this chapter of our human story, all marriages and families miss the mark of God's intentions for them. Some more than others. Nevertheless, we should think of them when we read Scriptures like these:

> The LORD is good to all,
> And his mercy is over all that he has made (Psalm 145:9)

> He makes his sun rise on the evil and on the good, and sends rain on the just and on the unjust. (Matthew 5:45)

> God's kindness is meant to lead you to repentance. (Romans 2:4)

> In past generations [God] allowed all the nations to walk in their own ways. Yet he did not leave himself without witness, for he did good by giving you rains from heaven and fruitful seasons, satisfying your hearts with food and gladness. (Acts 14:17)

Marriage and family are tokens of God's commitment to our well-being.[14] Even if God is not honored and thanked for his gifts, he gives them. Many enjoy them. The world benefits from them. Even if marriages and families wander from the path that God laid out for them, the world is a better place because of them.

JOY AFTER DIVORCE

Let's be honest. When we hold our marriages up to the straight edge of God's design for them, they are bent. Crooked. There are no exceptions. Even at their best, marriages that seek the glory of God fall far short of that lofty calling. There are not enough tears in the world for marriages that come to an end. No one enters marriage genuinely with its demise in view, but it happens, even for those who are followers of Christ. The glory of God is eclipsed by human failure. The possibilities of grace don't become realities. Instead there is disappointment, sorrow, frustration, anger, and pain. Vows are broken. Commitments are not honored. Or maybe the bond of love is simply too weak, and breaks beneath a burden of stress and the weight of the world. What began in faith, hope, and love ends in a painful parting of ways. I know some of these men and women. They are family and friends. We share life together in the same fellowship of faith. I grieve for them and confess that I am not one whit better.

If you are on the other side of divorce, how are these chapters relevant for you? You probably don't need to hear that God hates divorce,[15] but you may need to hear that he loves divorced people. There is only one unforgivable sin according to Jesus,[16] and it isn't divorce. Grace and mercy are offered to you. Will you accept them? Will you let them shape your life from this day on? Let me encourage you to thumb back through the pages of this book and re-learn the joys of salvation (in Chapter 4) and God's ability to bring good things from bad things (in Chapters 7 and 8). God takes us where we are and seeks to move us forward. We can't change our past, but the power of the past can be broken in ways that will change our future.[17] I don't know how God will write the rest of your story, but I know that you can trust him with the tale. In his goodness he desires what is best for you, in his wisdom he knows how to bring it about, and in his unlimited power he is able to do it.[18]

If you are on the other side of divorce and you have children from your former marriage, there are still important roles for you to play in their lives. Your children need your love: your nurturing and mentoring love, your friendship, and most of all the love of Christ through you.

Maybe you have remarried. Whether your divorce involved the unfaithfulness or abandonment of a spouse, or the embers of your love grew cold, I leave the moral factors in your divorce and remarriage in God's hands and your heart before him.[19] However you have come into your current marriage, I believe this to be true: God's plan for your life from this point on includes the marriage you are in. You should pursue everything we have talked about in this chapter and the two that precede it. If you have children from your earlier marriage, you still have a debt of love to them. It may have twists, turns, and complications that wouldn't otherwise have been factors in your life or theirs, but you must embrace them. If you are now in a blended family with stepchildren or children from this union, you have opportunities and responsibilities of love for your spouse and the children that are members of your household. Give yourself to these loves, and the joys of our gracious and merciful God can still be yours!

JOYFUL SINGLENESS

If you are single, what does our exploration of marriage and family have to do with you? If marriage is your hope and desire, my counsel to you is to pray daily for the man or woman that God may bring to you. What you don't know yet is fully disclosed to him. He knows that man, that woman, even if you don't. Pray and wait. Wait for the Lord. Wait for his timing. Let this ancient prayer be yours:

> But I trust in you, O LORD;
>   I say, "You are my God."
> My times are in your hand. (Psalm 31:14-15)

Pray that God will prepare this man or this woman for the four loves of marriage and family that we will explore in the next two chapters. As you seek the Lord and his good plan for your life, make these loves a focus of your prayer. Spend time with couples (young and old) in which you see these loves displayed. Learn from them.

If you are single, *please* wait for sex until you are married! Don't open that present until it is God's gift to you in marriage. Honor the marriage bed,[20] and God will honor you. It is worth the wait. I understand that our culture mocks chastity, but the Author of Life does not. He esteems it highly. Your commitment to him will be blessed in ways that are unknown to your peers. Your last laugh will be the best laugh, because it will be the laughter of joy. If, like many, you have fallen in this area of your life, it is as true for you today as it was when Jesus first spoke the words: *Repentance* is the doorway through which you must walk.[21] On the other side you will find grace, mercy, and the restored joys of salvation.[22]

Steward your singleness well. If you pursue joy, you will flourish in life as a single person, and bring your best to a marriage relationship. Cultivate your joy in God, his world, and his Word. Let the joy of salvation fill your heart. Develop joy in your work, joy in your play, joy in your creativity, and joy in your service for the Kingdom of God.

This is ironic but true: The greater your obsession with finding a spouse, the less you will be prepared for a healthy marriage. The more you focus on God-given joys in life before marriage and family, the greater your joy will be if and when God grants these relationships. If marriage and family exist for the glory of God, the best thing you can do is develop a passion for his glory in this God-appointed time of your life. Marriage should not be your purpose; that must be reserved for glorifying God and enjoying him. Make that your aim, and if God grants your request to be a husband or a wife, and a mother or a father, you will have stewarded your singleness well and prepared yourself to steward marriage and family life for his glory.

What about those who are not simply single, but celibate? All who are celibate are single,[23] but not all who are single are committed to a lifetime of celibacy. It is a special gift and a calling. Jesus spoke of it this way:

Not everyone can receive this saying, but only those to whom it is given. For there are eunuchs who have been so from birth, and there are eunuchs who have been made eunuchs by men, and there are eunuchs who have made themselves eunuchs for the sake of the kingdom of heaven. Let the one who is able to receive this receive it. (Matthew 19:10-12)

After encouraging the church of Corinth to consider the advantages of being single, Paul wrote: "Now as a concession, not a command, I say this. I wish that all were as I myself am. But each has his own gift from God, one of one kind and one of another."[24] Earlier in that discourse he spoke of married couples abstaining temporarily from sexual relations so that they could better devote themselves to prayer. People who have been gifted and called to be celibate make this commitment for a lifetime. Celibacy is giving up a good for a higher good. Marriage and family are good gifts from God, but the Kingdom of God is greater.[25]

If this gift and calling are yours, you have more time to devote to the Kingdom. In the next volume of *River of Delights* you will learn how you can become a joyful Kingdom activist. You will be able to do this in ways that your married friends cannot, and you will discover joys that will be yours alone.

QUESTIONS FOR THOUGHT AND DISCUSSION

1. How does the notion of vocation help you understand marriage and family?

2. How does holiness fit into your understanding of marriage and family? What difference would it make for you to see these relationships set apart for and consecrated to God and his purposes for the world?

3. Read the following quote about Martin Luther. "[His] faith was simple enough to trust that after a conscientious day's labor, a Christian father could come home and eat his sausage, drink his beer, play his flute, sing with his children, and make love to his wife — all to the glory of God!" How is this different from what you've heard about marriage and the glory of God?

4. If you have been divorced, or know someone who has been, what prospects for joy do you see? How can you pursue this for yourself or encourage others who are on the other side of divorce?

5. If you are single, or know someone who is, how will you pursue joy in this time of your life? How can you help others pursue joy and singleness?

CHAPTER 12

MARRIAGE AND FAMILY
LOVE'S DELIGHTS, PART 1

S *torge, philia, eros,* and *agape.* Ancient Greeks used these words to describe love. In English we would recognize them as *affection, friendship, being in love,* and *charity.*[1] When they are ours, these loves constitute a full, robust life. Together they hallow relationships and honor the God of love.[2]

These loves are essential to our joy. Josef Pieper wrote, "All love has joy as its natural fruit."[3] Joy is the beatitude of love. It is love's delight.[4] It is the pleasure of loving and being loved. In marriage and family these nuanced loves and their matching joys create a collage of pleasure that can't be found anywhere else. Only in these relationships can we experience all four loves and their delights without walking out our front door!

STORGE

C.S. Lewis saw *storge* as the humblest of the four loves that we will explore.[5] Its foundation is not shared interests (*philia*), or shared attraction (*eros*), but shared life. It is the bond that makes the familiarities of living together possible.   It is the relational warmth that emanates from embers of shared time and space, and the rhythms and routines of life. It is the affection of mothers and fathers for their children, children for their parents, and sisters and brothers for each other. It is the cord that binds family and clan together.

Storge delights in a first word, a first tooth, and a first step. It walks a child to first grade, cheers a first homerun, and records a first recital. *Storge* celebrates birthdays, weddings, anniversaries, and family vacations. It prays in a hospital waiting room, holds vigil when death is near, puts flowers on a grave, and enshrines family memories in stories passed from one generation to another.

While *philia, eros,* and *agape* can exist without *storge*, it is unlikely that they will develop fully without it.[6] As Lewis put it, "A plant must have roots below as well as sunlight above."[7] To change the metaphor, *storge* is an anchor and a sail. It provides security and creates opportunity. It crafts a stable setting in which children grow and develop in healthy ways (which is why the plight of orphans is dire, and why children in broken and incomplete homes can be disadvantaged in life).

In a Christian vision of life, *storge* begins with the affirmation that marriage and family relationships are gifts from God and find their meaning in relation to him:[8]

> Therefore a man shall leave his father and his mother and hold fast to his wife, and the two shall become one flesh. . . . *What therefore God has joined together*, let not man separate (Matthew 19:5-6)

> He who finds a wife finds a good thing, and obtains *favor from the LORD.* (Proverbs 18:22)

> Behold, children are a heritage *from the LORD,*
>   the fruit of the womb a reward.
> Like arrows in the hand of warrior

are the children of one's youth.
Blessed is the man who fills his quiver with them! (Psalm 127:4-5)

[*The LORD*] gives the barren woman a home,
    making her the joyous mother of children. (Psalm 113:9)

Fathers, do not provoke your children to anger, but bring them up
in the discipline and instruction *of the Lord*. (Ephesians 6:4)

Children, obey your parents *in the Lord*, for this is right. 'Honor
your father and mother' (this is the first commandment with a
promise), 'that it may go well with you and that you may live long
in the land.' (Ephesians 6:1-3)

Lewis described *storge* in unflattering terms:

> It is indeed the least discriminating of loves. There are women for
> whom we can predict few wooers and men who are likely to have
> few friends. They have nothing to offer. But almost anyone can
> become an object of Affection; the ugly, the stupid, even the
> exasperating. There need be no apparent fitness between those
> whom it unites. I have seen it felt for an imbecile not only by his
> parents but by his brothers. It ignores the barriers of age, sex, class
> and education. It can exist between a clever young man from the
> university and an old nurse, though their minds inhabit different
> worlds.[9]

There is another way of looking at this. *Storge* is an everyday love. It is love
wearing an apron, or work boots and gloves. It loves with or without merit.
It loves even the unlovely. It is a strong, durable love. A faithful, steady, and
unwavering love. *Storge* is an echo of God's parental love for us.[10] Like the
father in Jesus' parable of the prodigal son,[11] God loves us even when we
break his heart:

Children have I reared and brought up, but they have rebelled
against me. (Isaiah 1:2)

Can a woman forget her nursing child, that she should have no
compassion on the son of her womb? Even these may forget, yet I
will not forget you. (Isaiah 49:15)

When Israel was a child, I loved him,
    and out of Egypt I called my son.
The more they were called,
    the more they went away. . .
I led them with cords of kindness,
with the bands of love . . .
My people are bent on turn away from me. . .
How can I give you up, O Ephraim?
    How can I hand you over, O Israel? . . .
My heart recoils within me;
    My compassion grows warm and tender. (Hosea 11:1-8)

Like the fiercely devoted love of a mother, God's love for us never weakens,
never ceases:

Can a woman forget her nursing child,
    that she should have no compassion on the son of her womb?
Even these may forget,
    yet I will not forget you. (Isaiah 49:15)

Storge is the love of parents for children, even in their waywardness. It is the
love of children for parents, even with their shortcomings.[12]   Luther wrote:

It must therefore be impressed on young people that they revere
their parents as God's representatives,   and to remember that,
however lowly, poor, feeble, and eccentric they may be, they are

still their mother and father, given by God. They are not to be deprived of their honor because of their ways or failings.[13]

Storge loves simply because families are God's creation and this affection is his design for them. It is fuel to a furnace, wind to a sail, water to a mill.

If it is true to God's design, *storge* is a nurturing and mentoring love. When it was written of Jesus in his boyhood that he "increased in wisdom and in stature, and in favor with God and man,"[14] it is a tribute to this love. God designed the process, and chose and prepared the family in which Jesus would be shaped by years of affectionate home life.

Storge is a stewarding love, shaped by a charge from God. Luther wrote:

> The greatest good in married life, that which makes all suffering and labor worth while, is that God grants offspring and commands that they be brought up to worship and serve him. In all the world this is the noblest and most precious work.[15]

> If our dear God and Father in heaven grants you children, nurture and care for them, raise them up in the discipline, fear, and admonition of the Lord. Then you will be doing right and performing better and nobler good works than all the monks and nuns; then you will be living in God's vocation and ordinance.[16]

Family affection is the current that carries wisdom from one generation to another:

> Hear, O Israel: The LORD our God, the LORD is one. You shall love the LORD your God will all your heart and with all your soul and with all your might. And these words that I command you today shall be on your heart. You shall teach them diligently to your children, and shall talk of them when you sit in your house, and when you walk by the way, and when you lie down and when you rise. (Deuteronomy 6:4-7)

Hear, my son, your father's instruction,
  and forsake not your mother's teaching. (Proverbs 1:8)

Storge equips children to flourish in life before God. It prepares girls to become godlywise women, and, if God wills, wives and mothers. It prepares boys to become godlywise men, and, if God wills, husbands and fathers. *Storge* is fulfilled in the priestly role of parents praying for their children, bringing them daily before the throne of grace, asking God to guide and direct, to provide and protect, and then seeking to be an answer to those prayers.

A family shaped by this love becomes a classroom of character. In this little community of intimate relationships, where life in its many facets is played out every day, children learn virtue from their parents. They learn Christ-likeness. Mothers and fathers model Christ, and children benefit from their example. Parents tell children stories of virtue and live out their own. Children are praised for their progress, encouraged for their efforts, held accountable for their words and deeds, and forgiven when they fail. Day after day, week after week, month after month, year after year, hearts are formed by the constancy of this love.[17]

Storge is a multi-generational love, from the first cry of a baby to the seasoned wisdom of a family's seniors, from kinder care to hospice care. (Ours is the loss when grandparents value retirement in a warmer climate more than they do sharing life with their children and grandchildren. Ours is the loss when advancement in a career, with its many moves, is more important than letting our children grow up with the experience of elder love.[18] Ours is the loss when aunts, uncles, and cousins are only seen on Christmas cards.) There is a wealth in family love that truly enriches. Beautiful tapestries of life are woven from family experiences that span generations. The joys that accompany this love cannot be found anywhere else.

PHILIA

Philia, or friendship, is a congenial love. It is based upon common beliefs, values, interests, and concerns, and the mutual enjoyment of people who share these things. Lewis wrote, "Without Eros none of us would have been begotten and without Affection none of us would have been reared; but we can live and breed without Friendship."[19] True, but we don't live well without it. You can find *philia* among neighborhood children, schoolmates, colleagues, and professional peers. You can discover it in churches, social organizations, book clubs, athletic teams, choirs, and bands, but it is formative and foundational in our lives when we experience it in marriage and family.

In family life *philia* and *storge* often overlap, or flow together. If my wife teaches our children culinary skills (because they would learn little from me), it is an expression of *storge*. If they come to enjoy the kitchen as she does, and they delight in preparing food together, it is *philia* enriching *storge.* If I teach our children the lore of hiking in the Rockies, this is *storge* in a mentoring role. If they come to love the mountains as I do, and we enjoy exploring them together, it is *philia* adding its touch to *storge*. Parents and children become friends. Their affection is strengthened by this love and enhanced by its joys. Brothers and sisters who know this love become friends for life.

What about *philia* between a man and a woman? It is wondrous, with dangers lurking nearby! Lewis wrote:

> When the two people who thus discover that they are on the same secret road are of different sexes, the friendship that arises between them will very easily pass – may pass in the first half-hour – into erotic love. Indeed, unless they are physically repulsive to each other or unless one or both already loves elsewhere, it is almost certain to do so sooner or later.[20]

This is why it is dangerous to a marriage if a husband develops friendships with women other than his wife, or a wife with men other than her husband.[21] The power of our sexuality and the weakness of our fallen nature make us vulnerable. The same hazards exist for unmarried men and women when they "just want to be friends," but find that friendly affection pulled into sexual attraction whether it is their intent or not.

What if the friendship of a man and woman is fulfilled in marriage? It is cause for great celebration! It is expressed beautifully in the Song of Solomon: "This is my *beloved* and this is my *friend*."[22] *Philia* strengthens, deepens, and enriches a marriage relationship. When shared interests grow beyond children and the demands of nurture and provision, new pleasures and joys follow.[23] Shared worship, friendships, recreation, leisure, music, the arts, and social concern and action enhance married life. Couples who cultivate *philia* in their marriage discover joys in life that no other friends can know.

When *philia* is redeemed and shared, the common interests and concerns of friends center around joy in God, his world, his word, and his will.[24] Friendship at its highest and best includes friendship with Jesus.[25] When he is the Nexus in a relationship between friends, their joy includes his joy in them and theirs in him.

When *philia* is redeemed in marriages and families, they move closer to Eden. They are not yet all that God wants them to be, but they venture "further in and higher up"[26] than they can with *storge* alone. Husbands and wives, parents and children, sisters and brothers, truly enjoy each other. They don't merely share space under the same roof, they flourish in life together. When they are friends in Christ, some of the greatest joys that can be known become theirs.

QUESTIONS FOR THOUGHT AND DISCUSSION

1. How has *storge* played out in the family you grew up in? How was/is it expressed? Was/is it a strong or a weak force? How do you want to do things differently in your own marriage and family?

2. What kind of mentoring and nurturing love did you experience growing up? Do you think you were prepared for marriage and family life yourself? How so? How not? How do you want to do things differently?

3. How do you see television, movies, video games, and unsupervised internet use impacting *storge* in family life? What commitments will you make in light of your response to these questions?

4. If you are married, how would you evaluate *philia* between you and your spouse? If you are single, how did you see *philia* play out in your parents' relationship?

5. If you are a parent, how would you evaluate *philia* with your children, and *philia* among your children? If you aren't yet a parent, how would you evaluate *philia* in what you know of your parents' relationship, and your relationship with your siblings? What can you do to strengthen this love?

Chapter 13

Marriage and Family
Love's Delights, Part 2

Eros

*E*ros is what we mean when we talk about *being in love*.[1] It includes our sexuality, but it is more than this. It is possible to be familiar with the pleasures of sex and to be a foreigner to *eros*. Arranged marriages often include procreation and its pleasures without the presence of this love. The love of a husband and a wife, once robust with *eros,* can lapse into bedtime routines between emotional strangers. In our day, sex without *eros* has become epidemic among the unmarried. (Yes, I intended to say that. Keep reading and you will see why.) Unrestrained hedonism and mutual consent justify anything that can be imagined.

Popular opinion notwithstanding, *eros* and lust are not the same thing. Lust is fallen *eros*. It is a God-given desire that has been corrupted by our sin.[2] *Eros* is a flame lit by candles of desire and delight, attraction and admiration, enjoyment and esteem. Lust is a cold, calculating pursuit of pleasure. *Eros* is drawn to the beloved, desires the beloved, and is enraptured by the beloved. Lust seeks gratification. Period. C.S. Lewis wrote:

Sexual desire, without Eros, wants *it*, the *thing in itself*; Eros wants the Beloved. The *thing* is a sensory pleasure; that is, an event occurring within one's own body. We use a most unfortunate idiom when we say, of a lustful man prowling the streets, that he "wants a woman." Strictly speaking, a woman is just what he does not want. He wants a pleasure for which a woman happens to be the necessary piece of apparatus.[3]

Our confusion extends to marriage.[4] Husbands and wives can mistake lust for *eros*. If each uses the other for personal satisfaction, it is lust, not *eros*. If each is a taker and not a giver, it is lust, not *eros*. Couples who make this mistake believe that God approves because they once shared a wedding ceremony and now share life under the same roof. This way of thinking and acting degrades the gift of sex, demeans what God has made us to be as sexual beings, and despoils the sacred covenant of marriage.

Lust can be mistaken for *eros*. The opposite error occurs when *eros* is mistaken for lust. This happens when sex is framed by a dualistic understanding of the world in which the spiritual realm is good and the physical realm – as such – is evil. In this vision of life, sex is castigated as a "carnal" pleasure. At best it is a necessary evil in the service of procreation; at worst it turns our hearts away from God and perverts true love. You can find this view among ancient Christian theologians who were influenced by Plato and his followers.[5] Here are a few examples of this error:

> Our general argument concerning marriage, food, and other matters, may proceed to show that we should do nothing from desire. Our will is to be directed only towards that which is necessary. For we are children not of desire but of will. A man who marries for the sake of begetting children must practice continence so that it is not desire he feels for his wife, whom he ought to love, and that he may beget children with a chaste and controlled will.[6]
> *Clement of Alexandria (c. 150–215)*

"He who too ardently loves his own wife is an adulterer." It is disgraceful to love another man's wife at all, or one's own too much. A wise man ought to love his wife with judgment, not with passion.[7] *Jerome (c. 347 – 420)*

In a good marriage, even with older people, although the passion of youth between man and woman has waned, the relationship of love between husband and wife continues strong, and the better persons they are, the earlier they begin by mutual consent to abstain from carnal union.[8] *Augustine (354 – 430)*

The commandment 'go forth and multiply' does not necessarily mean through conjugal union. For God could increase the human race by another means, if people had preserved the commandment inviolable to the end.[9] *John of Damascus (c. 645 -749).*

There are many in our day who can't connect the dots between God and sex, or if they do, the marks form a frown. God must surely avert his eyes from husbands and wives in bed! But what if there is a smile on the face of God as he delights in married couples enjoying the pleasures he designed and has given to them? If lust and *eros* are not the same, surely this is possible! John Calvin wrote, "Satan dazzles us . . . to imagine that we are polluted by intercourse. . . . [But] when the marital bed is dedicated to the name of the Lord, that is, when parties are joined together in his name, and live honorably, it is something of a holy estate."[10] In a wedding sermon, Martin Luther wrote:

> God's word is actually inscribed on one's spouse. When a man looks at his wife as if she were the only woman on earth, and when a woman looks at her husband if he were the only man on earth; yes, if no king or queen, not even the sun itself sparkles any more brightly and lights up your eyes more than your own husband or wife [a wonderful description of *eros*], then right there you are face

to face with God speaking. God promises to you your wife or husband, actually gives your spouse to you saying, 'The man shall be yours. I am pleased beyond measure! Creatures earthly and heavenly are jumping for joy.'[11]

Eros includes our sexuality, but it is not first about sex. *Eros* is captivated and enchanted by the beloved. It longs for the beloved and delights in the beloved. [12]   In God's design for marriage, sex follows powerfully and inevitably from this love. *Eros* reaches its full stature when it is the pleasure of loving and being loved, when we love to love,[13] when we give from our joy for the sake of our beloved's joy, when pleasure is mutual and delight is shared.

We will explore playful joy in the next volume of *River of Delights*. It is enough to say here that play is a good gift from our good God. When *eros* is redeemed, sex (always and only in the sacred covenant of marriage) is love in a playful mode, engaged in a game in which each player seeks to out-give the other. Generosity is the measure of the game; pleasure-given-and-received is its prize. (In actual experience the giving and receiving are so thoroughly interlaced that it becomes impossible to distinguish them.)[14]

Eros-redeemed celebrates God's delight in our delight. It is a pleasure known to grateful hearts. In this way *eros* can become an expression of worship as much as any of his gifts that we offer back to him in thanksgiving and praise:

> Now the Spirit expressly says that in later times some will depart from the faith . . . who forbid *marriage* and require abstinence from foods that *God has created to be received with thanksgiving by those who believe and know the truth. For everything created by God is good, and nothing is to be rejected if it is received with thanksgiving, or it is made holy by the word of God and prayer.* (1 Timothy 4:1-5)

This puts us in the best position to understand *The Song of Solomon* and its inclusion in the canon of Scripture. It isn't an allegory. It is a celebration of *eros*. It revels in the enjoyment of sexual love. It is sex as sacred play. Even if the Ancient Near Eastern imagery seems strange to us, we are invited to affirm the goodness of husbands and wives delighting in each other before God:

> Let him kiss me with the kisses of his mouth!
> For your love is better than wine. . . (1:2)

> As an apple tree among the trees of the forest,
>   so is my believed among the young men.
> With great delight I sat in his shadow,
>   and his fruit was sweet to my taste.
> He brought me to the banqueting house,
>   and his banner over me was love.
> Sustain me with raisins,
>   refresh me with apples,
>   for I am sick with love.
> His left hand is under my head,
>   and his right hand embraces me! (2:3-6)

> You have captivated my heart, my sister, my bride;
>   you have captivated my heart with one glance of your eyes,
>   with one jewel of your necklace.
> How beautiful is your love, my sister, my bride!
> How much better is your love than wine,
>   and the fragrance of your oils than any spice! (4:9-10)

> How beautiful and pleasant you are,
>   O loved one, with all your delights!
> Your stature is like a palm tree,
>   and your breasts are like its clusters.

I say I will climb the palm tree
and lay hold of its fruit.
Oh may your breasts be like clusters of the vine,
and the scent of your breath like apples,
and your mouth like the best wine. (7:7-9)

Eros is good, because it is the gift of a good God. It is included in our joy, because it is the gift of a joyful God.

When *eros* is redeemed, sexual love is a reaffirmation of marital vows. Each time anew, sexual union embraces vows given and received in the presence of God on a couple's wedding day. It is a recommitment to their sacred covenant. Sexual love strengthens the bonds of marriage through giving and receiving, mutual fulfillment of God-given desires, and a shared pleasure in God and his good gifts.

When *eros* joins the voices of *storge* and *philia* in marriage, the trio echoes the ancient harmony of Eden. The coupling of a husband and wife before God becomes healthy, robust, and joyful, because it moves closer to God's design at the dawn of our creation.

AGAPE

We come at last to *agape*, the highest of the four loves.[15] In God's design, *storge, philia,* and *eros* prepare our hearts for this love. They are *agape's* early lessons:

From the first coupling of the parents in desire for each other and for fruit, through the carrying of the first child by the mother and the husband's consideration for his pregnant wife, on through the suckling and feeding, to the training of the children ("Say 'thank you,'" or "Pick up your paper dolls," or "Stand up when your mother comes into the room,") and the ordinary muddle of things done together, it is all the school of Charity. For is not Charity the name given to that final, perfect, gloriously free and blissful state where all the lessons have been so mastered that the *rules* ("Pick up your paper dolls," or "Thou shalt not steal") have withered, and all of us have won through to the capacity to experience as joy, the thing that was hinted at in all our early lessons; namely, that My Life For Yours *is* the principle at the bottom of everything, to embrace which is to live and to refuse which is to die?[16]

The true glory of *storge, philia,* and *eros* emerges when they bow before the highest love. They become most fully themselves and most fully offer their unique contributions to life when they do. As Lewis put it, "In this yoke lies their true freedom; they 'are taller when they bow.'"[17]

Agape is the most Godlike of the loves, because it is pure Gift-love. When we say that God is love,[18] and that he is the Giver of every good and perfect gift,[19] we are saying the same thing in different ways. In creation we see God's love as he "gives life and breath to all."[20] In redemption, he loves the world and gives his only Son.[21] The Son gives his life as a ransom for a world held hostage in sin.[22] The Spirit is given to us,[23] and he bestows the boon of his presence.[24] The Gifting-God loves to give. This is *agape*.

Agape is unconditional, but not invincible. It is the most powerful of the loves because of what it can accomplish; it is often the most tragic of the loves, because its aspirations are so high and it can be scorned. If we allow *agape* to shape our loves, we must accept the risk that comes with it:

There is no safe investment. To love at all is to be vulnerable. Love anything, and your heart will certainly be wrung and possibly be broken. If you want to make sure of keeping it intact, you must give your heart to no one, not even to an animal. Wrap it carefully round with hobbies and little luxuries; avoid all entanglements; lock it up safe in the casket or coffin of your selfishness. But in that casket, safe, dark, motionless, airless – it will change. It will not be broken; it will become unbreakable, impenetrable, irredeemable.

The alternative to the risk of tragedy, is damnation. The only place outside Heaven where you can be perfectly safe from all the dangers and perturbations of love is Hell.[25]

By his sovereign permission, even God's love can be unrequited.[26] He allows his love to be refused.[27] When it is, his heart is broken. There is love-rejected in the poignant words of Jesus as he stands *in loco Dei*,[28] addressing the Holy City: "O Jerusalem, Jerusalem, the city that kills the prophets and stones those who are sent to it! How often would I have gathered your children together as a hen gathers her brood under her wings, and you were not willing!"[29]

Even if it can be spurned, *agape* is the most potent of the loves. It is *agape*, and only *agape*, that can save our world. It is a love expressed most powerfully in the cross of Christ:[30] "For while we were still weak, at the right time Christ died for the ungodly. For one will scarcely die for a righteous person—though perhaps for a good person one would dare even to die – but God shows his *love* for us in that while we were still sinners, Christ died for us."[31] There is no greater love than this. Christ did not die for the godly (there are none), or for those with merit (a class without members), but for those who deserve only judgment (all of us). The Righteous One gave his life for an unrighteous world.[32] This is the greatest love our world can know. The river of redemption has its headwaters here.

Agape can transform our lives because it transforms our loves and renovates their domains in life. *Agape* changes *storge's* ordinary love between family members into something extraordinary. It infuses families with a power to love when loving would not be their normal response. *Agape* brings with it the other fruit of the Spirit: joy, peace, patience, kindness, goodness, faithfulness, gentleness, and self-control,[33] and these virtues of love shape every facet of marriage and family life.

Agape can transform *philia*: "Greater *love* has no one than this: than to lay down one's life for one's *friends*."[34] When this happens, friends not only enjoy common interests and enjoy each other, they share a common commitment: Each would give his or her life for the other. Imagine a family in which a woman knows that her husband would gladly die for her, a man knows that his wife would willingly give her life for him, and children know that their parents would surrender their lives for them without hesitation or hint of regret. There is no stronger bond of friendship. There are no stronger families than those who share this love.

Agape can transform *eros*. The paradox of hedonism is that the more you seek pleasure, the more it goes bad on you. But this is only true if the pleasure you are seeking is your own! There is a very different paradox in play when *agape* transforms *eros*: The more you seek the pleasure of your beloved, the greater your pleasure, and the greater your joy. "I am my beloved's, and my beloved is mine."[35] This is *eros*. It is a good gift. *Eros* needs the beloved, can't bear to live without him, cannot endure without her. *Agape* raises *eros* to a higher level when it says, "I am my beloved's, my beloved is mine, and we are God's." He becomes the apex of their relationship, the highest point that their love together can reach.

Inscribed in the Bible that was given to me by my wife more than twenty-five years ago are these words:

Dearest Rick,

For my husband who points me to Christ each day by the life he lives. My love through His,

Sue

"My love through His." *Agape* is the most Godlike of the loves, but there is more to it than this. God "communicates to men a share of His own Gift-love."[36] He loves through us. We love through his love. *Agape* integrates our loves and transposes them into something higher and better. Transformed by *agape, storge, philia* and *eros* are ennobled and enriched by God's touch. They are empowered by his love coursing through them.

Joy is love's delight.[37] When joy is the beatitude of the four loves in the richly colored and textured relationships of marriage and family, there is no other beauty like it in our world. No other fragrance has its allure. The joys of *storge, philia, eros,* and *agape,* experienced in day-to-day life in marriages and families, bring us as close to Eden as we will get in this chapter of the human story.

The spiritual significance of marriage and family can be easily missed because we are so close to these relationships, so caught up in them. There is great power in these words:

> I would like to suggest that at least one place (among others) which may be hallowed anew as the place where all the celebration of all the mysteries may occur, and where all of life may be offered up in oblation to the Most High, is the family household. Within these four walls, under this roof, the lamps are lighted. The offering is here, the vigil is here, the feast is here, the faithful are here. All the eating and drinking, and the working and playing, and the discipline and serving and loving that go on here – they are all holy. For these common routines of ordinary life are not only necessities and functions: they are also messengers to us from the hallows. Nay, more than messengers, they *are* those hallows, set hourly before us in visible, touchable, light-of-day forms.[38]

"O God, bring these truths into our marriages and our families! Bring these loves! Make them realities in our lives! What we receive from you we offer back to you in worship. These relationships, these loves, this joy, we offer to the world for its greater good and your greater glory. Amen."

QUESTIONS FOR THOUGHT AND DISCUSSION

1. After reading this chapter, how is lust different from *eros*, and how does that challenge views you have held?

2. Read the following quote.

   > There are many in our day who cannot connect the dots between God and sex, or if they do, the marks form a scowl or at least a frown. God must surely avert his eyes from husbands and wives in bed! But what if the dots form a smile on the face of God as he delights in married couples enjoying the pleasures that he himself designed and has given to them?

   How does viewing *eros* as a good gift from our good God challenge your understanding of this love?

3. In what ways can *agape* redeem *storge*, and what would that look like in your life?

4. In what ways can *agape* redeem *philia*, and what would that look like in your life?

5. In what ways can *agape* redeem *eros*? What implications does this have for you. How could this change our culture?

About the Author

I n 1983 Rick and Sue Howe moved to Boulder, Colorado, where they raised three children – Amberle, Lorien, and Jamison – and have devoted more than thirty years to campus ministry at the University of Colorado. In addition to writing and speaking, Rick now leads University Ministries, whose mission is to "inspire and nurture a thoughtful pursuit of Christ, one student, one professor, one university at a time." To learn more about Rick, visit his website at www.rickhowe.org. You can also follow him on Facebook at *Rick Howe on Joy* and on Twitter @rickhoweonjoy. To learn more about University Ministries, see www.university-ministries.org.

ENDNOTES

PREFACE

Proverbs 17:22

Dallas Willard, *Renovation of the Heart: Putting on the Character of Christ* (Colorado Springs, CO: NavPress, 2002), p. 133.

Peter Kreeft, *Heaven: The Heart's Deepest Longing* (San Francisco: Ignatius Press, Expanded Edition, 1980), p. 129.

CHAPTER 1: ENJOYING GOD

See "The Highest and Best of All Pleasures" in Rick Howe, *Path of Life: Finding the Joy You've Always Longed For* (Boulder, CO: University Ministries Press, 2017).

"With you is the fountain of life; in your light do we see light." (Psalm 36:9, NRSV)

Aquinas wrote: "When they desire any good whatsoever, whether by intellective, sensitive, or unconscious appetite, all things desire God as their end, for nothing attracts but for some likeness to God." *St. Thomas Aquinas: Philosophical Texts*, ed. and trans. Thomas Gilby (Durham, North Carolina: The Labyrinth Press, 1982), p. 130.

Augustine wrote, "But when you enjoy a human being in God, you are really enjoying God rather than the human being. You will be enjoying the one, after all, in whom you find your bliss." Saint Augustine, "Teaching Christianity" in *The Works of Saint Augustine: A Translation for the 21ˢᵗ Century*, trans. Edmund Hill (Hyde Park, NY: New City Press, 1996), p. 122.

Whether it is traced to its Source or not, we enjoy the "fragrance of the knowledge of Christ." See 2 Corinthians 2:14 – "But thanks be to God, who in Christ always leads us in triumphal procession, and through us spreads the fragrance of the knowledge of him everywhere."

If you read *Path of Life*, you may remember these words from Chapter 4, "The Joy of the Lord." Howe, *Path of Life,* p. 48

Augustine, "The Confessions," in *Basic Writings of Saint Augustine* , ed., Whitney J. Oates (Grand Rapids: Baker Book House, 1980), Vol. I, p. 3. I have modernized the English translation.

[8] Pascal, *Pascal's Pensées*, trans. W.F. Trotter (New York: E.P. Dutton & Co., Inc., 1958), p. 113.

[9] *"Delight yourself in the LORD*, and he will give you the desires of your heart."   (Psalm 37:4)

[10] Jonathan Edwards wrote: "[True saints] first rejoice in God as glorious and excellent in himself, and then secondarily rejoice in it, that so glorious a God is theirs." Jonathan Edwards, "On Religious Affections," *The Works of Jonathan Edwards,* Perry Miller, Gen. ed., (New Haven: Yale University Press, 1959), Vol. 2, pp. 249-50.

[11] Augustine wrote, of God, "Thou art an everlasting joy to Thyself!" St. Augustine, "Confessions," in *The Basic Writings of Saint Augustine,* ed., Whitney J. Oates (Grand Rapids: Baker Book House, 1948, repr. 1980), p. 114. According to Aquinas, God "possesses joy in Himself and all things else for His delight." And, "God is happiness by His Essence: for He is happy not by acquisition or participation of something else, but by His Essence." Aquinas, *Summa Theologica,* trans. Fathers of the English Dominican Province (London: Burns Oates & Washburn, Ltd., third ed. 1941), I, Q. 26, A. 1., and I, II, Q. 3., A. 1.

For a development of this theme, see "The Joy of the Lord" in Howe, *Path of Life.*

[12] Edwards wrote, "The first foundation of the delight a true saint has in God, is his own perfection; and the first foundation of the delight he has in Christ, is his beauty; he appears in himself the chief among ten thousand, and altogether lovely." Jonathan Edwards, "On Religious Affections," pp. 249-50.

[13] Ibid.

[14] Bruce Demarest quotes Morton Kelsey: "In Protestantism, God became a theological idea known by inference rather than a reality known by experience." He then adds: "Through a 'left-brain' approach to the faith, God easily becomes an abstraction removed from lived experience. A.W. Tozer noted that even as many scientists lose God in His world . . . so many theologians lose God in His Word." Bruce Demarest, *Satisfy Your Soul* (Colorado Springs: NavPress, 1999), p. 96.

[15] See Isaiah 6:1-5, NRSV.

[16] Psalm 34:8, RSV

[17] For the larger context of this hymn, see the verses before and after:

> For just as you were at one time disobedient to God but now have received mercy because of their disobedience, so they too have now been disobedient in order that by the mercy shown to you they also may now receive mercy. For God has consigned all to disobedience, that he may have mercy on all. (Romans 11:31-32)

I appeal to you therefore, brothers, by the mercies of God, to present your bodies as a living sacrifice, holy and acceptable to God, which is your spiritual worship. (Romans 12:1)

18 "And before him no creature is hidden, but all are open and laid bare to the eyes of him with whom we have to do." (Hebrews 4:13, RSV).

19 Psalm 90:14, NRSV

The experience of God was so vivid to hearts that poets used the language of perception to describe it. For example, see Psalm 17:15; 25:15; 26:3; 27:4.

20 See also Micah 7:18; Luke 10:21, NASB; 12:32.

21 I explore the sorrow of God in "The Joy of the Lord" in *Path of Life.* In brief, God's joy is found in who he is and what he does; his sorrow is a response to who we have become, and what we do, in our sin.

22 Dallas Willard, *The Divine Conspiracy: Rediscovering Our Hidden Life in God* (Harper Collins Publishers: San Francisco, 1998), p. 61.

23 John 15:11

24 This is what the apostle Paul meant, I think, when he said that we "have the mind of Christ." (1 Corinthians 2:16). It is thinking about things the way Christ would.

25 Mark 9:24.

26 Theologians make a distinction between the "ontological" Trinity and the "economic" Trinity. The ontological Trinity refers to God as he exists in himself. It is who God is. The economic Trinity refers to what this God does, and how he makes himself known in the world and the affairs of human beings (The word "economic" is from the Greek *oikonomikos,* signifying the arrangement of activities and affairs in a household.) My explanation of the how the Trinity came to be known and understood among early followers of Jesus falls under the rubric of the economic Trinity. This is not the old error of modalism, which says that the Father, Son, and Holy Spirit, are three modes in which the one God reveals himself. God reveals himself as a Trinity because he is a Trinity.

27 When Jewish people were asked who their God was, they told the stories of Abraham, Isaac and Jacob, and the God who was revealed to their ancient forefathers. When Christians were asked what deity they worshiped, they, too told a story: "Ours is the God of Israel, who has now made himself known uniquely and consummately in Jesus the Messiah, and in the Spirit poured out upon our Messianic community." They found their own story, and their understanding and experience of God, in this Story. It was not a theological dissertation. (The term *Trinitas* did not come into being until the early third century.) It was a tale that leapt to life in their encounter with God.

28 See, for example, Matthew 6:9.

29   Although it was not a major theme in his teaching or in the Jewish Scriptures which shaped his teaching, Jesus used feminine images (but not feminine titles) for God. These, too, connect with our experience of God. In the trilogy of parables about something lost and found (a sheep, a coin, a son) in Luke 15, the one who seeks what is lost represents God: a shepherd, a woman, and a father. When he spoke the following words, he drew from the Old Testament tradition of likening God's parental love for his people to mothers in the animal world:

> O Jerusalem, Jerusalem, the city that kills the prophets and stones those who are sent to it! How often would I have gathered your children together as a hen gathers her brood under her wings, and you were not willing! (Matthew 23:37)

For its Old Testament background, see Deuteronomy 32:10-12; Ruth 2:12; Psalm 17:8; 57:1; Hosea 13:4-8. God is also pictured as a human mother. See Isaiah 42:14; 49:15; 66:13.

30   I understand that much of the language of "sonship" with respect to Jesus has to do with his role as Messiah. But Jesus himself used it in ways that went beyond that. See, e.g., Matthew 11:26-28 and Luke 10:21-23, and the sonship of Jesus throughout the Gospel of John.

31   John 15:11. See also John 17:13, NRSV: "But now I am coming to you; and I speak these things in the world, so that they may have my joy made complete in themselves."

32   Peter Kreeft, *Heaven: The Heart's Deepest Longing* (San Francisco: Ignatius Press, Expanded Edition, 1980), p. 159.

33   It put them into a state of "cognitive dissonance," as contemporary psychologists might describe it.

34   See the following: 1 Peter 2:22; 2 Corinthians 5:21; 1 John 3:5.

35   See Mark 1:21-22.

36   See: Mark 2: 1-11.

37   See, for example: Matthew 11:27; John 10:30; 14"10-11' 20:17.

38   See, for example, Mark 2:23-28.

39   See Matthew 7:21-23; 25:31-37.

40   C.S. Lewis famously wrote:

> I am trying here to prevent anyone saying the really foolish thing that people often say about Him: I'm ready to accept Jesus as a great moral teacher, but I don't accept his claim to be God. That is the one thing we must not say. A man who was merely a man and said the sort of things Jesus said would not be a great moral teacher. He would either be a lunatic – on the level with the man

who says he is a poached egg – or else he would be the Devil of Hell. You must make your choice. Either this man was, and is, the Son of God, or else a madman or something worse. You can shut him up for a fool, you can spit at him and kill him as a demon or you can fall at his feet and call him Lord and God, but let us not come with any patronizing nonsense about his being a great human teacher. He has not left that open to us. He did not intend to.

C.S. Lewis, *Mere Christianity* (New York: Macmillan, 1952), pp. 55-56. For a recent defense of this argument, see David A. Horner, "*Aut Deus aut Malus Homo:* A Defense of C.S. Lewis's 'Shocking Alternative,' in *C.S. Lewis as Philosopher: Truth, Goodness and Beauty*, eds., David Baggett, Gary R. Habermas and Jerry L. Walls (Downers Grove, IL: InterVarsity Press, 2008).

[41]   If it hadn't been revealed to them, they could never have guessed it or reasoned their way to it. See Matthew 11:25-27.

[42]   See: Acts 2:1-4.

[43]   See John 14:16-17.

[44]   Compare these passages: John 14:16-17, 18; 2 Corinthians 3:17-18; 4:5. Luke T. Johnson writes, "This Holy Spirit is not an impersonal force; it is the life-giving presence of the risen Lord." Luke T. Johnson, *The New Testament Writings: An Interpretation* (Philadelphia: Fortress Press, 1986), p. 107.

[45]   See Acts 2:13.

[46]   See Acts 1:8.

[47]   See Luke 24:49.

[48]   See: John 14:16-18, 26.

[49]   See John 14:25-26; 16:13-14.

[50]   See Ephesians 1:13-14.

[51]   See Romans 8:14-16.

[52]   See, for example, Acts 13:52; 1 Thessalonians 1:6; Galatians 5:22-23; Romans 14:17.

[53]   2 Corinthians 13:14.   See also Matthew 28:19.

For "triadic" references to God in New Testament writings, see Ephesians 4:4-6; 1 Corinthians 12:3-6; 1 Peter 1:2; Ephesians 1:3-1.

For passages in which all three Persons are mentioned together, see Mark1:10-11; Galatians 4:4-6; Romans 8:1-4; 2 Thessalonians 2:13-17; Titus 3:4-6 Jude 20-21.

54   J.N.D. Kelly wrote:

> The doctrine of one God, the Father and creator, formed the background and indisputable premiss of the Church's faith. Inherited from Judaism, it was her bulwark against pagan polytheism, Gnostic emanationism and Marcionite dualism. The problem for theology was to integrate with it, intellectually, the fresh data of the specifically Christian revelation. Reduced to their simplest, these were the convictions that God had made Himself known in the Person of Jesus, the Messiah, raising Him from the dead and offering salvation to men through Him, and that He had poured out His Holy Spirit upon the Church. Even at the New Testament stage ideas about Christ's pre-existence and creative role were beginning to take shape, and a profound, if often obscure, awareness of the activity of the Spirit in the Church was emerging. No steps had been taken so far, however, to work all these complex elements into a coherent whole. The Church had to wait for more than three hundred years for a final synthesis. . . . of one God existing in three co-equal Persons. . . ."

J.N.D. Kelly, *Early Christian Doctrines*, Fifth Edition (London, New York NY: Continuum International Publishing Group, 2000), p. 87.

55   Augustine, "On Christian Doctrine," p. 524.

Following Augustine, the Catholic theologian, M.J. Scheeben, wrote:

> When God graciously adopts us as His children and truly unites us to Himself in a most intimate manner by the grace of sonship . . . He gives us Himself, His own essence, as the object of our delight. . . . In consequence of this presence of the divine essence in the soul and the real union of the soul with God which is effected by grace . . . we enjoy God . . . as an object that is really and truly in us and is our own. We truly grasp Him with our knowledge and embrace Him with our love . . . . God becomes the object of our possession and enjoyment in His entire essence. Evidently, then, all three persons come to us and give themselves to us, inasmuch as they are one with the essence, and in the essence with each other. Yet the individual persons, too, as distinct from one another and especially so far as one proceeds from another, can give themselves to us for our possession and enjoyment.

Quoted in Edmund J. Fortman, S.J., *The Triune God: A Historical Study of the Doctrine of the Trinity* (Philadelphia: The Westminster Press, 1972), p. 306.

56   For a contemporary call to ground our lives as Christians in the Triune life of God, see Jeff Imbach, *The River Within: Loving God, Living Passionately* (Colorado Springs: NavPress, 1998).

For a philosophical treatment of the Trinity in human experience, see David Brown, *The Divine Trinity* (LaSalle, Illinois: Open Court Publishing Company, 1985), pp. 207ff.

CHAPTER 2: JOY AND THE GLORY OF GOD

1   See Acts 7:2.

2   See Psalm 24:7.

3   See Ephesians 1:17.

4   See 2 Peter 1:17.

5   If you read *Path of Life*, you may remember this section on the glory of God from the chapter, "Joy and the Good Life."   Rick Howe, *Path of Life: Finding the Joy You've Always Longed For* (Boulder, CO: University Ministries Press, 2017).

The Westminster Shorter Catechism tells us that there are two dimensions of our chief end – glorifying God and enjoying him. We do not have two chief ends, but one with two facets (as John Piper observes in his work, *Desiring God: Meditations of a Christian Hedonist* [Portland, Oregon: Multnomah Press, 1986], p. 13. As C.S. Lewis saw it, "Fully to enjoy is to glorify. In commanding us to glorify Him, God is inviting us to enjoy Him." C.S. Lewis, *Reflections on the Psalms* [New York: Harcourt Brace Jovanovich, 1958], p. 97.)

Glorifying God and enjoying him are united in our life before him, because glory and joy are united in God himself. Karl Barth was right:

> God's glory is the indwelling joy of His divine being which as such shines out from Him, which overflows in its richness, which in its super-abundance is not satisfied with itself but communicates itself.

> God's glory is His overflowing self-communicating joy. By its very nature it is that which gives joy.

> But we cannot overlook the fact that God is glorious in such a way that He radiates joy.

Karl Barth, *Church Dogmatics*, eds., Geoffrey W. Bromiley, T. F. Torrance (New York: Charles Scribner's Sons, 1957), Vol. II, pp. 647, 653, 655.

6   Bernard Ramm calls it "both a modality of the self-revelation of God, and an attribute of God." Bernard Ramm, *Them He Glorified* (Grand Rapids: Eerdmans, 1963), p. 10. Karl Barth wrote: "[God's glory] is God Himself in the truth and capacity and act in which He makes himself known as God." Barth, *Church Dogmatics*, Vol. II, p. 641.

7   See John 4:24.

8   1 Timothy 1:17, RSV

[9] See 1 Timothy 6:16.

[10] For the metaphor of God robing himself, see: Psalm 93:1; 102:25-26; 104:1-2. Calvin quoted this last Psalm and then wrote:

> It is as if he said; Thereafter the Lord began to show himself in the *visible splendor of his apparel,* ever since in the creation of the universe he brought forth those insignia *whereby he shows his glory to u*s, whenever and wherever we cast our glaze. (Emphasis added.)

John Calvin, *Institutes of the Christian Religion,* ed., John T. McNeill, trans. Ford Lewis Battles (Philadelphia: Westminster, 1960), Vol. 1, p. 52.

[11] God appears to mortals in his glory. See, for example, Psalm 102:15-16.

[12] Deism is the view that a supreme being created the universe, but does not interfere in its workings, choosing, instead, to let it run entirely "on its own" according to the laws of nature imbedded in it from its origin.

[13] Pantheism is the view that the world and God are identical. If we could see beyond illusions and deceptive appearances we would see that everything is divine.

[14] The word "panentheism" literally means "everything-in-God-ism." It is the view that although there is a dimension to God which transcends the cosmos, the cosmos is part of God and exists in God.

[15] The universe is "charged with the grandeur of God." Gerard Manley Hopkins, "God's Grandeur," in *Chief Modern Poets of Britain and America,* ed., Gerald DeWitt Sanders, John Herbert Nelson, M.L. Rosenthal (London: The Macmillan Company, 1970), Vol. I, p. 60.

John Walton sees the creation account in Genesis portraying the cosmos as a temple in which God comes to dwell, and through which he makes his glory known. John H Walton, *The Lost World of Genesis One: Ancient Cosmology and the Origins Debate,* (Downers Grove, IL: InterVarsity Press, 2009).

The world as the theater of God's glory was a significant theme in the thought of John Calvin. See "John Calvin and the World as a Theater of God's Glory" in Belden C. Lane, *Ravished by Beauty: The Surprising Legacy of Reformed Spirituality* (Oxford: Oxford University Press, 2011), pp. 57-85.

[16] See Romans 1:25.

[17] Quoted in *The Essential Augustine,* ed., Vernon J. Bourke (Indianapolis: Hackett Publishing Company, second printing, 1978), pp. 131-132.

[18] In the Scriptures, glory and beauty are often closely related. See, for example, Exodus 28:2; 1 Chronicles 16:29, KJV; Isaiah 28:5.

19   St. Augustine, "Sermon 241," *The Works of Saint Augustine,* III/7, p. 71.

20   Theologians created a word for this: *theophany,* or a visible manifestation of God.

21   See Exodus 3:1-6.

22   See, for example, Exodus 14:19-20; 24:15-17.

23   See Exodus 19:16; 20:18-19; 2 Samuel 22:14-15.

24   See Exodus 40:34.

25   Jewish rabbis used the word "Shekinah" to describe the glory of God in his dwelling among humans. See Gerhard Kittel, ed., *Theological Dictionary of the New Testament,* trans. Geoffrey W. Bromiley (Grand Rapids, MI: Wm. B. Eerdmans Publishing Co., 1964), Vol. II, pp. 245-46.

26   In addition to the theme of divine glory in the Scriptures, we should add God's spoken word. He speaks in many ways (Hebrews 1:1). It may be an audible voice or an inner word. He may speak in a dream or a vision. His word may come to us directly, or through someone else he brings into our lives. Just as we hold ourselves in a state of readiness for glory, we should anticipate ways in which God may address us with a word. The posture of our hearts throughout the day ought to be, "Speak, LORD, for your servant is listening." (1 Samuel 3:9)

27   See 2 Corinthians 1:3; 11:31; Ephesians 1:3.

28   In the Hymn, *This is My Father's World,* we sing, "In the rustling grass I hear him pass." Not all grass that moves in the wind bears his presence to us, but it can and might!

29   Psalm 40:16

30   See, for example Jeremiah 29:13; Proverbs 8:17; Hebrews 11:6.

31   Exodus 33:18-19, NRSV. 2 Peter 1:3 links the glory of God and the goodness of God: "His divine power has given us everything we need for a godly life through our knowledge of him who called us by his own glory and goodness." (NIV)

32   Ramm, *Them He Glorified,* pp. 20-21.

33   See Psalm 27:4, RSV.

34   Jürgen Moltmann, *Theology and Joy,* trans. Reinhard Ulrich (London: SCM Press, LTD, 1973), p. 62. Speaking of joy and the beauty of God, Karl Barth wrote: "He has it as a fact and a power in such a way that He acts as the One who gives pleasure, creates desire and rewards with enjoyment, because He is the One who is pleasant, desirable, full of enjoyment, because first and last He alone is that which is pleasant, desirable and full of enjoyment." Barth, *Church Dogmatics,* Vol. II, Part 1, p. 651.

35 A.W. Tozer, *Whatever Happened to Worship?* ed., Gerald B. Smith (Camp Hill, Pennsylvania: Christian Publications, 1985), p. 28.

You may wonder why I include theologians who, apart from their interest in joy, have little in common. Moltmann and Tozer? Joy is a gift that is given without respect to theological conventions. It has the potential to unite people despite their theological differences. Joy is an ecumenical force. Those who experience joy do their best to describe it with the theological grammar and vocabulary at hand.

36 2 Corinthians 3:18

37 Jonathan Edwards, "Dissertation Concerning The End for Which God Created the World," in *The Works of Jonathan Edwards* (Philadelphia: The Banner of Truth Trust, 1984), Vol. I, p. 101.

38 See 2 Corinthians 3:18.

39 See 2 Corinthians 3:8.

40 See Acts 9:1-9.

41 See 2 Corinthians 4:6, RSV.

42 See Isaiah 6:3.

43 See 1 Peter 1:8.

44 See Psalm 19:1.

45 See 2 Corinthians 3:18.

46 1 Peter 1:8

47 The Incarnation itself is the greatest Divine Visitation. The reality of Incarnation ("This is my Son, whom I love; with him I am well pleased.") was disclosed dramatically in this episodic Visitation.

48 But not after it. As great as the glory of the Transfiguration must have been, the glory of the risen and ascended Christ is far greater! The apostle Paul was blinded by it (Acts 9:1-9), and John fell as a dead man after his encounter with it (Revelation 1:9-20).

49 In a story placed just before the Transfiguration, Jesus had this very important conversation with his disciples:

> Now it happened that as he was praying alone, the disciples were with him. And he asked them, "Who do the crowds say that I am?" And they answered, "John the Baptist. But others say, Elijah, and others that one of the prophets of old has risen." Then he said to them, "But who do you say that I am?" And Peter answered, "The Christ of God." (Luke 9:18-20)

[50] See John 1:14.

CHAPTER 3: ENJOYING GOD'S WORLD

[1]   ". . . when the morning stars sang together
       and all the sons of God shouted for joy?" (Job 38:7)

This inspired C.S. Lewis in his story of the creation of Narnia. In *The Magician's Nephew*, Lewis wrote:

> In the darkness something was happening at last. A voice had begun to sing. It was very far away and Digory found it hard to decide from what direction it was coming. Sometimes it seemed to come from all directions at once. Sometimes he almost thought it was coming out of the earth beneath them. Its lower notes were deep enough to be the voice of the earth herself. There were no words. There was hardly even a tune. But it was, beyond comparison, the most beautiful noise he had ever heard. It was so beautiful he could hardly bear it. . . .
>
> Then two wonders happened at the same moment. One was that the voice [of Aslan] was suddenly joined by other voices; more voices than you could possibly count. They were in harmony with it, but far higher up the scale: cold, tingling, silver voices. The second wonder was that the blackness overhead, all at once, was blazing with stars. They didn't come out gently one by one, as they do on a summer evening. One moment there had been nothing but darkness; next moment a thousand, thousand points of light leaped out – single stars, constellations, and planets, brighter and bigger than any in our world. There were no clouds. The new stars and the new voices began at exactly the same time. If you had seen and heard it, as Digory did, you would have felt quite certain that it was the stars themselves which were singing, and that it was the First Voice, the deep one, which had made them appear and made them sing.

C.S. Lewis, *The Magician's Nephew* (New York: NY, HarperTrophy, 1983), pp. 116-117.

[2]   In Anselmian terms, God is that than which no greater can be conceived. He is supreme in every conceivable way.

[3]   "He was free to create or not to create. He did it out of his own good pleasure, for the divine fun of it." Louis Smedes, "Theology and the Playful Life," in *God and the Good: Essays in Honor of Henry Stob*, eds., Clifton Orlebeke and Lewis Smedes (Grand Rapids: William B. Eerdmans Publishing Co. 1975), p. 56.

We see the Creator's joy in his creative work first in his benedictions over it: "And God saw that it was *good.*" (Genesis 1:10, 12, 18, 21, 25, 31)

[4]   See, for example, Psalm 103:1-5; 107:9; James 1:17.

[5]   See "The Highest and Best of All Pleasures" in Rick Howe, *Path of Life: Finding the Joy You've Always Longed For* (Boulder, CO: University Ministries Press, 2017). My primary thesis there is that joy is the highest and best of life's pleasures, and the one Pleasure that embraces and enhances all other pleasures given by God.

6   Martin Luther, *The Table Talk of Martin Luther*, ed., Thomas S. Kepler (Grand Rapids: Baker Book House, 1952, reprint., 1979), pp. 40-41.

7   Peter Kreeft, *Heaven: The Heart's Deepest Longing* (San Francisco: Ignatius Press, 1989), p. 111.

8   See also Acts 17:27-28, RSV; Romans 1:20, RSV.

9   See Psalm 139:7-12.

10   For a recent treatment of the immanence of God as the presence and work of the Spirit, see Clark Pinnock, *Flame of Love: A Theology of the Holy Spirit* (Downers Grove, Illinois: InterVarsity Press, 1996), especially chapter 2.

11   Calvin wrote:

> Men cannot open their eyes without being compelled to see him. Indeed, his essence is incomprehensible; hence, his divineness far escapes all human perception. But upon his individual works he has engraved unmistakable marks of his glory. . . . ever since in the creation of the universe he brought forth those insignia whereby he shows his glory to us, whenever and wherever we cast our gaze.

John Calvin, *Institutes of the Christian Religion*, ed., John T. McNeill, trans. Fort Lewis Battles (Philadelphia: The Westminster Press, 1960), Vol. I, p. 52.

12   C.S. Lewis, *Letters to Malcolm: Chiefly on Prayer* (New York: Harcourt Brace Jovanovich, Inc., 1963), pp. 89-90.

13   C.S. Lewis wrote: "God whispers to us in our pleasures, speaks in our conscience, but shouts in our pains." C.S. Lewis, *The Problem of Pain*, New York: Collier Books, Macmillan Publishing Company, 1962), p. 93.

14   Luther, *Table Talk*, p. 67. Emphasis added.

15   John Calvin, *Institutes of the Christian Religion*, trans. Henry Beveridge (Grand Rapids: William B. Eerdmans Publishing Co., 1979), Vol. I, p. 157. Emphasis added.

16   Nicholas Wolterstorff, *Art in Action: Toward a Christian Aesthetic* (Grand Rapids: William B. Eerdmans Publishing Co., 1980), p. 72.

17   Arthur F. Holmes, *Contours of a World View* (Grand Rapids: William B. Eerdmans Publishing Co., 1983), p. 67.

18   C.S. Lewis, *Mere Christianity* (New York: Macmillan Publishing Co., Inc., 1960 ed.) p. 65.

19   C.S. Lewis, "The Weight of Glory" in *The Weight of Glory and Other Addresses* (Grand Rapids: William B. Eerdmans Publishing Co., 1949, reprint. 1974), p. 14.

20 "Man is neither angel nor brute." *Pascal's Pensées*, trans. W.F. Trotter, (New York: E.P. Dutton & Co., Inc., 1958), p. 99.

21 "I fancy the 'beauties of nature' are a secret God has shared with us alone. That may be one of the reasons why we were made. . . ." C.S. Lewis, *Letters to Malcolm: Chiefly on Prayer* (New York: Harcourt Brace Jovanovich, Inc., 1963), p. 18.

Elsewhere Lewis wrote:

> The angels have not senses; their experience is purely intellectual and spiritual. That is why we know something about God which they don't. There are particular aspects of His love and joy which can be communicated to a created being only by sensuous experience. Something of God which the seraphim can never quite understand flows into us from the blue sky, the taste of honey, the delicious embrace of water whether cold or hot, or even from sleep itself.

C.S. Lewis, "Scraps" in *God in the Dock: Essays on Theology and Ethics* (Grand Rapids: William B. Eerdmans Publishing Co., 1975), p. 216.

22 While I acknowledge that contemporary genetic evidence and other postulates of evolutionary theory represent a challenge that should engage Christians in serious thinking and dialogue, I did not come to my belief (nor will I abandon my belief) in an historical Adam and Eve, an original Edenic environment in which they lived, and a state of innocence from which they fell, on the basis of scientific inquiry.

The Scriptures are the "norming norm" for my faith. I make no apologies for this. Indeed, it is a great joy to me! Having said this, the ancient texts of Scripture must be read first – as much as possible – with their original audience in mind. We should resist the temptation of importing our interests and concerns into the way we understand them, and forcing them to take up arms in our conflicts.

I recognize that the Hebrew word *adam* was used for humanity as a whole as well as for an individual in the Genesis story (Adam = Mankind). I can also see how Israel, in its exile from the promised land, would have seen itself in Adam and his expulsion from the Garden (Adam = Israel). Neither of these observations, however, negates the possibility that Adam was *also* viewed as an historical figure. (Compare Jacob = Israel.) Neither seems to factor into the canonical context of Jesus' teaching on marriage and divorce in Matthew 19, and Paul's exposition of redemptive history in Romans 5 – both of which posit an historical Adam.

While Jesus does not refer to an original pair by name, his affirmation of the Creator's original intention for marriage clearly has the Edenic couple in mind. ("He who created them from the beginning made them male and female, and said, 'Therefore a man shall leave his father and his mother and hold fast to his wife, and the two shall become one flesh.'" On the matter of divorce, he affirms an original state of innocence from which humanity has lapsed ("From the beginning it was not so.")
In Romans 5, Israel as a nation is not in view. The "one man" (Adam) is distinguished from all who followed from him ("all men"). In this passage we do observe the Jewish penchant for seeing deeper meanings in their stories. Adam is not an archetype for

humanity or for Israel, however, but a "type" of Christ. This is the frame of reference in which we should pursue our interpretation. The parallels are between two men (Adam and Christ), sin entering the world through one and grace through the other, an act of disobedience and an act of righteousness, judgment and justification, death and eternal life. Any other frame of reference is alien to the context. In a grand metanarrative, Paul lays out the themes of Creation, Fall, and Redemption: one man in the beginning from whom humanity sprang and through whose "act of disobedience" sin entered the world, an historical period ("from Adam to Moses"), and God's saving action through the one man, Jesus Christ ("the one who was to come").

I affirm that there is great value in the scientific enterprise, and believe that if we love God with our minds (in fulfillment of the greatest commandment) we will boldly declare that all truth is his – wherever it is found – and we will pursue it to the best of our abilities under God. I also affirm the priority and supremacy of the Scriptures for our faith, and what seems to me to be the clear teaching of Jesus and Paul. This leads me to a confident belief that whatever we may say about the age of the universe and the development of life on our planet, there was an original couple who bore the image of God without flaw, were placed in an Edenic setting of innocence, fell from that state through a primal act of disobedience, and brought sin into the world as well as all future generations of humans who fallibly bear the image of God.

For a contemporary discussion, see Matthew Barrett and Ardel B. Caneday, eds. *Four Views on the Historical Adam* (Grand Rapids: Zondervan, 2013).

[23]   See, for example, Ecclesiastes 2:1-11; Luke 8:14; 1 Timothy 5:6; 2 Timothy 3:4; Titus 3:3.

[24]   Augustine, "Confessions" in *The Basic Writings of Saint Augustine,* ed., Whitney J. Oates (Grand Rapids: Baker Book House, 1948, reprinted 1980), p. 179. I have changed the King James pronouns and verbal endings to a contemporary idiom.

[25]   C.S. Lewis, *The Problem of Pain* , pp. 79-80.

[26]   See 1 Timothy 4:1-2.

[27]   1 Timothy 4:4-5, NASB

[28]   C.S. Lewis, *Letters to Malcolm*, p. 89

[29]   Although it is incomplete because its only factors are creation and fall, Emil Brunner is worth quoting: "Since Creation comes first, and sin comes second, the primary duty of man is to adopt a positive attitude towards life - an attitude of affirmation, acceptance, and adjustment to its claims; the negative attitude of denial takes thesecond place." Emil Brunner, *The Divine Imperative,* trans. Olive Wyon, (The Westminster Press: Philadelphia, 1947), p. 126.

[30]   See, for example, Isaiah 65:17-19; 2 Peter 3:12-13; Revelation 21:1.

[31] Diogenes Allen captured the essence of this tension:

> To forsake the world is not to reject the world. To forsake the world is to realize that there is nothing you know of, have experienced, or can imagine, which would satisfy you.

> This attitude is perfectly compatible with a recognition of the glories of the world, its radiant beauty, its delights, its satisfactions, its wonders, and all the rest.

> Forsaking the world is an attitude. That is, it can exist alongside laughter, hearty fun, delight in a child, a full and active life. It does not drive everything else out, as does a mood. It does not rob things of value.

Diogenes Allen, *Finding Our Father* (Atlanta: John Knox Press, 1974), pp. 78-79.

Karl Barth captures something of this dialectic of "yes" and "no" in our joy:

> What is here regarded as joy, and is this, has obviously passed through a catalysator. It has been destroyed on the one hand, and reconstituted on the other. But it has been reconstituted, and validated, and even raised to the level of a command. Christ is risen; He is truly risen. Joy is now joy before the Lord and in Him. It is joy in His salvation, His grace, His law, His whole action. But it is now genuine, earthly, human joy: the joy of harvest, wedding, festival and victory; the joy not only of the inner but of the outer man; the joy in which one may and must drink wine as well as eat bread, sing and play as well as speak, dance as well as pray.

Karl Barth, *Church Dogmatics*, trans., Mr. A.T. Mackay, et. al. (Edinburgh: T. & T. Clark, 1961) Volume III, 4, pp. 375-376.

[32] This is another way of saying, as Aquinas did, that there is a rational, as well as a sensory dimension, to human pleasure:

> Pleasure arises from union with a suitable object perceived or known.

> Three things are requisite for pleasure; two, i.e., the one that is pleased and the pleasurable object conjoined to him; and a third, which is knowledge of this conjunction.

Thomas Aquinas, *Summa Theologica* I, II, Q. 31, A. 5 and Q. 32. A. 1.

[33] St. Augustine, "City of God" in *Basic Writings of Saint Augustine*, ed. Whitney J. Oates (New York: Random House Publishers, 1948) Vol. II, p. 108. Emphasis added.

[34] Aquinas, *Summa Theologica*, I, I, Q. 5, A.4. Emphasis added.

[35] David Elton Trueblood, *Philosophy of Religion* (Grand Rapids: Baker Book House, 1957), p. 120. Emphasis added.

[36] C.S. Lewis, *Letters to Malcolm*, pp. 89-90.

[37] See Romans 1:18-28.

[38] Martin Luther, "Lectures on Genesis," in *Luther's Works*, ed., Jaroslav Pelikan (Saint Louis: Concordia Publishing House, 1960), Vol. II, p. 348.

[39] "Do not be conformed to this world, but be transformed by the renewal of your mind, that by testing you may discern what is the will of God, what is good and acceptable and perfect." (Romans 12:2)

[40] 1 Timothy 4:3-5.

[41] We live out our days enveloped by the *sacramentum mundi* (the sacrament of the world, or the world as sacrament.)

[42] John Walton sees the creation account in Genesis portraying the cosmos as a temple in which God comes to dwell, and through which he makes his glory known. John H Walton, *The Lost World of Genesis One: Ancient Cosmology and the Origins Debate*, (Downers Grove, IL: InterVarsity Press, 2009).

The world as the theater of God's glory was a significant theme in the thought of John Calvin. See "John Calvin and the World as a Theater of God's Glory" in Belden C. Lane, *Ravished by Beauty: The Surprising Legacy of Reformed Spirituality* (Oxford: Oxford University Press, 2011), pp. 57-85.

For explorations of stewarding the earth in a Christian vision of life, see: Steven Bouma-Prediger, *For the Beauty of the Earth: A Christian Vision for Creation Care* (Grand Rapids, MI: Baker Academic, 2001); Wesley Granberg-Michaelson, ed., *Tending the Garden: Essays on the Gospel and the Earth* (Grand Rapids, MI: Eerdmans, 1987); James A. Nash, *Loving Nature: Ecological Integrity and Christian Responsibility* (Nashville: Abingdon, 1993); Francis A. Schaeffer, *Pollution and the Death of Man: The Christian View of Ecology* (Wheaton, IL: Tyndale House, 1970); Loren Wilkinson, ed., *Earthkeeping in the '90s: Stewardship of Creation* (Grand Rapids, MI: Eerdmans, 1990) .

[43] With future generations in mind, our responsible use of the world's resources should include renewable energy as much as possible. It is tragic not only when we, through our governments, rack up debts that will crush future generations, but when we deplete the resources of the earth, leaving future generations in peril. We should oppose both economic policies and energy policies that endanger those who come after us.

[44] See Matthew 22:36-40.

CHAPTER 4: THE JOY OF SALVATION

[1]   A literal rendering of the name of the Garden in *The Septuagint*, the ancient Greek Translation of the Hebrew Scriptures.

[2]   Karl Barth wrote of God and creation, "Although he did not create it divine, He did not create it ungodly, or anti-godly, but in harmony and peace with Himself, and therefore, according to His plan, as the theatre and instrument of His acts, an object of His joy and for participation in this joy." Karl Barth, *Church Dogmatics*, eds., G.W. Bromiley, T.F. Torrance (London, New York: T & T Clark International, 2004), Vol. 3.1, p. 102.

[3]   C.S. Lewis, *Mere Christianity* (New York: Macmillan Publishing Co., Inc., 1960 ed.), p. 52. Emphasis added.

Peter Van Inwagen writes:

> Human beings have not been made merely to mouth words of praise or to be passively awash in a pleasant sensation of the presence of God. They have been made to be intimately aware of God and capable of freely acting on this awareness; having seen God, they may either glorify and enjoy what they have seen -- the glorification and the enjoyment are separate only by the intellect in an act of severe abstraction -- or they may reject what they have seen and attempt to order their own lives and to create their own objects of enjoyment. The choice is theirs and it is a free choice: to choose either way is genuinely open to each human being.

> God wishes to be the object of human glorification and enjoyment not out of vanity, but out of love: He is glorious and enjoyable to a degree infinitely greater than that of any other object. He has given us free will in this matter because it is only when a person, having contemplated the properties of something, freely assents to the proposition that that thing is worthy of glory, and then proceeds freely to offer glory to it, that a thing is truly glorified. And it is only when a person, having enjoyed a thing, freely chooses to continue in the enjoyment of that thing that true enjoyment occurs.

Peter Van Inwagen, "Non Est Hick" in *The Rationality of Belief & the Plurality of Faith*, Thomas D. Senor, ed., (Ithica and London: Cornell University Press, 1995), pp. 220-221.

[4]   It may be true, as Shakespeare put it, that "to err is human," but this is only true of us in our fallenness. We must never understand this to be the case with humanity-as-created-by-God.

[5]   Psalm 16:4, RSV

[6]   See Jeremiah 2:10-13.

7   See 1 Timothy 6:10.

8   See Ecclesiastes 2:1-10.

9   Peter Kreeft, *Heaven: The Heart's Deepest Longing* (San Francisco: Ignatius Press, Expanded edition, 1980), p. 21.

10 See Genesis 3:5.

11 Ephesians 2:3

12 The wrath of God is more than this. It includes his hatred of sin, his anger towards sin, and his judgment of sin. In Romans 1, however, God, in his wrath, withdraws and leaves us with the consequences of his absence and the presence of our sin. With finality, that is what hell will be. The result of wrath for us is the loss of joy, and that is the worst of all possible punishments!

13 Kreeft, *Heaven*, p. 135.

14 See Matthew 8:12.

15 See Psalm 16:11.

16 See 2 Thessalonians 1:9.

17 The sorrow of hell is unending because the sin of choosing another god is ongoing. C.S. Lewis wrote: "I willingly believe that the damned are, in one sense, successful, rebels to the end; that the doors of hell are locked on the inside." C.S. Lewis, *The Problem of Pain* (New York: Macmillan, 1962), p. 127.

18 C.S. Lewis wrote:

> There are only two kinds of people in the end: those who say to God, "Thy will be done," and those to whom God says, in the end, "Thy will be done." All that are in Hell, choose it. Without that self-choice there could be no Hell. No soul that seriously and constantly desires joy will ever miss it. Those who seek find. To those who knock it is opened.

C.S. Lewis, *The Great Divorce* (San Francisco: HarperCollins, 2001), p. 75.

19 See Psalm 51:12.

20 See Romans 5:5.

21 Robert Kolb and Timothy J. Wenger eds. *The Book of Concord: The Confessions of the Evangelical Lutheran Church*, trans. Charles Arand, et al (Minneapolis: Fortress Press, 2000), p. 23.

22 Jürgen Moltmann asks this question, and finds its answer in the freedom, good will and love of God. See Jürgen Moltmann, *Theology and Joy*, trans. Reinhard Ulrich (London: SCM Press, 1973), pp. 47ff.

23 Micah 7:18

24 Luke 12:32. "The Kingdom of God stands as a comprehensive term for all that the messianic salvation included." George Eldon Ladd, *A Theology of the New Testament* (Grand Rapids: William B. Eerdmans Publishing Co., 1974), p. 72.

25 Luke 15:7, 23-25, RSV

26 Hebrews 12:2, RSV

27 Hebrews 2:10, 14-15, NRSV

28 See Philippians 2:13.

29 See John 3:1-8.

30 2 Corinthians 5:17

31 A.W. Tozer, *Whatever Happened to Worship?* ed., Gerald B. Smith (Camp Hill, Pennsylvania: Christian Publications, 1985), p. 25.

The Heidelberg Catechism captures this sense of joy as well. It asks, "What is the birth of the new self?" And then answers, "Complete joy in God through Christ and a strong desire to live according to the will of God in all good works." "The Heidelberg Confession," in *The Book of Confessions* (United States: The General Assembly of the United Presbyterian Church in the United States of America, 1967). Q. 90.

32 C.S. Lewis wrote, "For this tangled absurdity of a Need . . . which never fully acknowledges its own neediness, Grace substitutes a full, childlike and delighted acceptance of our Need, a joy in total dependence. We become 'jolly beggars.'" C.S. Lewis, *The Four Loves* (New York: Harcourt, Brace, Jovanovich, 1960), p. 180.

33 C.S. Lewis, *Mere Christianity*, p. 52.

34 Luke 1:46-47

35 C.S. Lewis' way of describing the Trinity. See Chapter 24, "The Three-Personal God" in his *Mere Christianity*.

36 Josef Pieper wrote, "All love has joy as its natural fruit." Josef Pieper, *About Love* (Chicago: Franciscan Herald Press, 1974), p. 71. David Gill speaks of joy as "love's delight." See David W. Gill, *Becoming Good: Building Moral Character* (Downers Grove, Illinois: InterVarsity Press, 2000), p. 54.

37 Jonathan Edwards, "On Religious Affections," *The Works of Jonathan Edwards*, Perry Miller, Gen. ed., (New Haven: Yale University Press, 1959), Vol. 2, p. 114.

38   C.S. Lewis, *God in the Dock: Essays on Theology and Ethics,* ed., Walter Hooper (Grand Rapids: Eerdmans Publishing Co., 1970, reprint., 1976), p. 112.

39   C.S. Lewis, *The Weight of Glory and other Addresses* (Grand Rapids: Eerdmans Publishing Co., 1949, reprint. 1974), p. 14.

40   1 Peter 1:8. NASB

41   See Romans 5:2-3.

42   Hebrews 6:5

43   Jonathan Edwards, "On Religious Affections," p. 113.

44   See Romans 8:23; 1 Corinthians 15:44.

45   Ephesians 1:14.   See also 2 Corinthians 1:22, RSV.

46   See Romans 8:23.

47   The notion of justification should be understood in this framework. It is the verdict of the eschatological judgment rendered in advance because of what Christ has already done. We are declared righteous now in anticipation of the judicial pronouncement that will be made at the end of days.

48   Hebrews 11:16

49   Hebrews 12:22

50   Hebrews 6:5

51   Galatians 1:4

52   George Eldon Ladd, *A Theology of the New Testament* (Grand Rapids, MI: William B. Eerdmans Publishing Co., 1974) p. 69.

53   2 Corinthians 6:9-10

54   See 1 Corinthians 2:6-8.

55   See 1 Corinthians 15:20.

      Speaking of the resurrection of Christ, Moltmann says, "Here indeed begins the laughing of the redeemed, the dancing of the liberated . . . even if we still live under conditions with little cause for rejoicing." (*Theology and Joy*, p. 50)

56   From "A Mighty Fortress is Our God."

[57] This is the joy which Madeleine L'Engle sees captured in the Sanskrit word, *ananda*: "that joy in existence, without which the universe will fall apart and collapse." Madeleine L'Engle, *A Swiftly Tilting Planet* (New York, NY: Dell Publishing, 1979), p. 40. It is the joy that binds Being to being, and all created things to each other. It is the aim of creation and redemption alike.

John Calvin wrote:

> [The] Psalmist calls upon irrational things themselves, the trees, the earth, the seas, and the heavens, to join in the general joy. Nor are we to understand that by the heavens he means the angels, and by the earth men; for he calls even upon the dumb fishes of the deep to shout for joy. . . . As all elements in the creation groan and travail together with us, according to Paul's declaration, (Rom. 8:22) they may reasonably rejoice in the restoration of all things according to their earnest desire.

John Calvin, *Commentary on the Book of Psalms*, trans. Rev. James Anderson (Grand Rapids, MI: Baker Book House, reprint, 1979), Vol. IV, p. 58.

[58] Quoted in Moltmann, *Theology and Joy*, p. 57.

[59] Cornelius Plantinga writes:

> The prophets knew how many ways human life can go wrong because they knew how many ways human life can go right. (You need the concept of a wall on a plumb to tell when one is off.) These prophets kept dreaming of a time when God would put things right again.
>
> They dreamed of a new age in which human crookedness would be straightened out, rough places made plain. The foolish would be made wise and the wise, humble. They dreamed of a time when the deserts would flower, the mountains would run with wine, weeping would cease and people could go to sleep without weapons on their laps. People would work in peace and work to fruitful effect. Lambs could lie down with lions. All nature would be fruitful, benign, and filled with wonder upon wonder; all humans would be knit together in brotherhood and sisterhood; and all nature and all humans would look to God, walk with God, lean toward God and delight in God. Shouts of joy and recognition would well up from valleys and seas, from women in streets and from men on ships.
>
> The webbing together of God, humans, and all creation in justice, fulfillment, and delight is what the Hebrew prophets call *shalom*. We call it peace, but it means far more than mere peace of mind or a cease-fire between enemies. In the Bible shalom means *universal flourishing, wholeness, and delight* – a rich state of affairs in which natural needs are satisfied and natural gifts are fruitfully employed, a state of affairs that inspires joyful wonder as its Creator and Savior opens doors and welcomes the creatures in whom he delights. Shalom, in other words, is the way things ought to be.

Cornelius Plantinga, Jr., *Not the Way It's Supposed to Be: A Breviary of Sin*, (Grand Rapids, MI: William B. Eerdmans Publishing Company, 1995), pp. 9-10.

CHAPTER 5: JOY AND THE WORD OF GOD

[1] *The Table Talk of Martin Luther*, ed., Thomas S. Kepler (Grand Rapids: Baker Book House, 1952, reprint., 1979), p. 15.

[2] See also Psalm 1:1-2; 19:7-10.

[3] In my view, it is a mistake to think of distinct faculties as if they were separate from and independent of each other but somehow exist together in the same person. They are woven together in a single fabric. We are intellectual, emotional, volitional beings. Our health and ability to flourish in life are linked to these three dimensions of our inner life working in harmony.

[4] William Alston writes:

> Thus we are not afraid of x unless we take x to be dangerous; we are not angry at x unless we take x to be acting contrary to something we want; we do not have remorse over having done x unless we regard it as unfortunate that we did x; we are not grief-stricken over x unless we see x as the loss of something we wanted very much; we do not have pity for x unless we take x to be in an undesirable state; and so on.

William P. Alston, "Emotion and Feeling," in *The Encyclopedia of Philosophy*, ed., Paul Edwards (New York: Macmillan Publishing Co., 1967), Vol. II, pp. 479ff.

[5] Robert C. Roberts, *Spirituality and Human Emotion*, (Grand Rapids: Williams B. Eerdmans Publishing Co., 1982), p. 26.

[6] Louis Pojman has written, "All experiencing takes place within the framework of a world view. . . . What we see depends to some degree on our background beliefs and our expectations. The farmer, the real estate agent, and the artist looking at the "same" field do not see the *same* field." See his article, "A Critique of Gutting's Argument from Religious Experience" in Louis P. Pojman, ed., *Philosophy of Religion: An Anthology* (Belmont, CA: Wadsworth Publishing Co., 1987), pp. 139-140.

[7] Roberts contends that emotions "are no less tied to concepts than arguments and beliefs are." (*Spirituality*, pp.10, 21.) It is also important to affirm the other side of the coin, that emotions are central to worldviews (in the way they actually function in our lives). We are cognitive and affective beings, and the two are woven together. We are more than thinking beings (Descartes); there is no such thing as reason alone (Kant).

[8] Roberts also writes that "The Christian emotions . . . (e.g., love, joy, peace) are ways of 'seeing' which are determined by the peculiar Christian concepts and the scheme of

beliefs which give rise to those concepts." Ibid., p. 10. And, "They are "concerned ways of viewing things through the 'lenses' of Christian teaching." Ibid., p. 25.

[9] Paul L. Holmer, "Blessedness" in *Baker's Dictionary of Christian Ethics*, ed., Carl F.H. Henry (Grand Rapids: Baker Book House Co., 1973), p. 66.

Jonathan Edwards wrote, "Holy affections are not heat without light; but evermore arise from some information of the understanding, some spiritual instruction that the mind receives, some light or actual knowledge." Jonathan Edwards, "On Religious Affections" in *The Works of Jonathan Edwards,* Perry Miller, Gen. ed., (New Haven: Yale University Press, 1959), Vol. 2, p. 281.

[10] Roberts writes, "The gospel message provides people with a distinctive way of construing the world; the maker of the universe is your personal loving Father and has redeemed you from sin and death." Roberts, *Spirituality,*p. 16.

[11] Josef Pieper, *About Love,* trans., Richard and Clara Winston (Chicago: Franciscan Herald Press, 1974), p. 73. Before him, Aquinas called joy the "delight which follows reason." Thomas Aquinas, *Summa Theologica,* trans. Fathers of the English Dominican Province (London: Burns Oates & Washburn, Ltd., third ed. 1941), I, II, Q. 31, A. 3. I would only add that joy follows reason when reason is illumined by theological insight.

[12] The fact that joy is perspectival does not make it merely subjective. The fact that we can and do experience joy is evidence that the perspective is true! It fits the world that we live in.

[13] This is not to say that we can't learn truth about God-in-his-self-disclosure outside the Scriptures. We can, and it is glorious! Whatever is learned there, however, is learned more fully and clearly in the inspired Word. Many of the truths that frame and fill our joy can only be found here.

[14] Romans 15:13

[15] God's Word to us includes, but is more than, the Scriptures. The Bible itself tells us that God speaks in many ways, (Hebrews 1:1-2), and records a great variety of ways in which God has spoken over the millennia. In Paul's paradigmatic example of faith in his letter to the Romans (chapter 4), Abraham responds to God's word to him, hundreds of years before sacred scribes began their work. The principle, however, is the same in every age: Faith embraces God's Word – however it comes to us – with an affirming, trusting heart. Therein lies joy.

[16] Sometimes, in this fallen world, joy and the discovery of truth have a different relationship. What if the truth you discover is that you have cancer and have one year to live? There is still joy to be found here, but it will lie in discovering the greater truths of what God is seeking to do in and through this crisis, in his presence with you as you walk through the valley of the shadow of death, and in Paul's insight: "For this light momentary affliction is preparing for us an eternal weight of glory beyond all comparison." (2 Corinthians 4:17)

17   Augustine, "The Confessions" in *Basic Writings of Saint Augustine*, ed., Whitney J. Oates (Grand Rapids: Baker Book House, 1980), Vol. I, p. 164. I have changed the King James pronouns and verbal endings to a contemporary form.

18   This is the deeper truth behind Paul's statement that love "rejoices with the truth." (1 Corinthians 13:6)

19   C.S. Lewis, *Letters to Malcolm: Chiefly on Prayer* (New York: Harcourt, Brace & World, Inc.: 1964), pp. 89-90.

20   It was the hubris of the Enlightenment to think that we can reason our way objectively and certainly to truth about the world. It is the hubris of postmodernism to think that truth is entirely the construction of a community, and entirely relative to it.

21   See Arthur F. Holmes, *All Truth is God's Truth* (Grand Rapids: Willliam B. Eerdmans Publishing Co., 1977).

22   Augustine "Teaching Christianity" in *The Works of Saint Augustine: A Translation for the 21ˢᵗ Century*, ed. John E. Rotelle, O.S.A., trans. Edmund Hill, O.P. (New York: New City Press, 1996), I/11, p. 144.

23   John Calvin, *Institutes of the Christian Religion*, trans. Henry Beveridge (Grand Rapids: Willliam B. Eerdmans Publishing Co., eighth print., 1979), Vol. I, pp. 40-41.

24   Ibid., p. 236.

25   John Calvin, *Institutes of the Christian Religion*, ed., John T. McNeill, trans. Ford Lewis Battles (Philadelphia: Westminster, 1960), Vol. 1, p. 82.

26   This is the literal rendering of the Greek word, *theopneustos*, usually translated, "inspired by God" in 2 Timothy 3:16.

27   It was the error of Neo-orthodoxy to limit revelation to the personal disclosure of God. "God in his Word does not speak 'something true,' but himself . . ." And "what God wills to give us cannot really be given in words, but only in manifestation. . . ."Emil Brunner, *Truth As Encounter* (Philadelphia: The Westminster Press, 1964), pp. 132, 131. It is the Fundamentalist error to limit biblical revelation to propositional truth. Both camps are right in what they embrace and wrong in what they exclude.

   Revelation is no bare incursion of the Transcendent into the realm of space and time. If it were it would have no meaning for us. It would not be a *personal* encounter, but impersonal. According to Colin Brown:

> It is true that our personalities cannot be compressed into propositions. It is also true that unless we express ourselves in language, our attempts to express ourselves become a dumb charade. To deprive a person of language and the capacity to make himself articulate is to make that person sub-personal. There is no *a priori* reason why the personal God should not be able to express Himself in personal language. And the biblical writers attest this.

Quoted in Ronald H. Nash, *The Word of God and the Word of Man* (Grand Rapids: Zondervan Publishing House, 1982), p. 46.

It is in the propositional dimension of revelation that God sovereignly and graciously supplies us with the meaning of his self-disclosure. It is an equal and opposite error to reduce biblical revelation to bare propositions, however significant they may be. That would indeed be "bibliolatry," as detractors of evangelical Christianity often allege.

28   Acts 7:38

29   1 Peter 1:23

30   Emille Cailliet, *Journey into Light* (Grand Rapids: Zondervan Publishing House, 1968), p. 18.

Ronald Nash gives this very relevant word of caution to evangelical Christians:

> God's revelation is not static or dead; it is a gracious *act* of God. Evangelicals must beware lest their emphasis on revelation inscripturated in human language should degenerate into a de-emphasis of the living and active nature of God's speaking. The God whose voice can raise the dead is not one who can be limited by "dead" words. The activity of the Spirit of God insures the vitality of God's revelation. God speaks and His word is recorded. He continues to speak through that record; and those words live, energized by the Spirit of God.

Ronald Nash, *The Word of God and the Mind of Man*, p. 52.

31   Donald G. Bloesch, *A Theology of Word and Spirit* (Downers Grove, Illinois: InterVarsity Press, 1992), pp. 13-14.

32   J.I. Packer wrote:

> The joy of Bible study is not the fun of collecting esoteric tidbits about Gog and Magog, Tubal-cain and Methuselah, Bible numerics and the beast, and so on. . . . Rather, it is the deep contentment that comes of communing with the living Lord into whose presence the Bible takes us – a joy which only His own true disciples know.

J.I. Packer, *God Has Spoken* (Downers Grove: InterVarsity Press, 1979), p. 10.

33   The spiritual discipline of meditation includes more than a deep reflection on the Scriptures. We can meditate on God himself (Psalm 63:6; 145:5), his works in creation (Psalm 143:5), his deeds in history (including our own lives Psalm 77:12; 119:27; 143:5), as well as on anything that is true, honorable, just, pure, lovely, commendable, excellent, and praiseworthy (Philippians 4:8).

In this chapter my interest is in meditation on the Word of God. Here are a few passages that teach the practice of biblical meditation: Joshua 1:8; Psalm 1:2; 119:15, 23.

34 See Psalm 51:6.

35 Edwards, "On Religious Affections" in *The Works of Jonathan Edwards*, Vol. 2, p. 272.

36 Romans 12:2, NASB.

37 See the hymn, "Break Thou the Bread of Life," by Mary A. Lathbury.

38 Walter C. Kaiser, Jr., "What is Biblical Meditation?" in *Renewing Your Mind in a Secular World*, ed., John D. Woodbridge (Chicago: Moody Press, 1985), 50.

CHAPTER 6: ENCOUNTERING GOD IN HIS WORD

1 Most importantly, let me encourage you to develop a consistent practice of reading the Scriptures interactively. Train yourself to ask questions like these as you read:

> ➤ Is there worship for me to join?
> ➤ Is there a prayer for me to offer?
> ➤ Is there a promise for me to embrace?
> ➤ Is there a blessing for which I can be thankful?
> ➤ Is there a truth for me to affirm?
> ➤ Is there wisdom for me to make my own?
> ➤ Is there a sin for me to avoid?
> ➤ Is there a vice for me to resist?
> ➤ Is there a command for me to obey
> ➤ Is there a virtue for me to cultivate?

Lists like this have circulated in various forms for years. This list of questions is one I created for my own ministry of discipleship.

2 "Divine reading" or "Spiritual reading." Although I draw from classic forms of *lectio divina*, this chapter reflects ways in which I have practiced and experienced them in relevant and fruitful ways.

3 Protestant Christians may be surprised to learn that *lectio divina* developed as a tradition in the Roman Catholic Church, inspired by Saint Benedict.

For helpful studies, see the following: David G. Benner, *Opening to God: Lectio Divina and Life as Prayer* (Downers Grove, IL: IVP Books, 2010); Christine Valters Paintner, Lucy Wynkoop, OSB, *Lectio Divina: Contemplative Awakening and Awareness* (New York, Mahwah, NJ: 2008); M. Basil Pennington, *Lectio Divina: Renewing the Ancient Practice of Praying the Scriptures* (New York: Cross Road Publishing, 1998); Raymond

Studzinski, *Reading to Live: The Evolving Practice of Lectio Divina*, (Collegeville, MN: Liturgical Press, 2009.

See also: Richard J. Foster, with Kathryn A. Helmers, *Life with God: Reading the Bible for Spiritual Transformation* (New York, NY: HarperCollins, 2008); Evan B. Howard, *Praying the Scriptures: A Field Guide for Your Spiritual Journey* (Downers Grove, IL: InterVarsity Press, 1999); Eugene H. Peterson, *Eat This Book: A Conversation in the Art of Spiritual Reading* (Grand Rapids, MI: Wm. P. Eerdmans Publishing Co., 2006); Peter Toon, *The Art of Meditating on Scripture: Understanding Your Faith, Renewing Your Mind, Knowing Your God* (Grand Rapids, MI: Zondervan Publishing House, 1993).

[4] Because of the time commitment involved in doing a full *lectio divina*, it may be something you do on special occasions to supplement your daily interaction in the Word. However, the more adept you become with this discipline, the more you will be able to practice parts in many different settings, with much time or little.

The spiritual art and discipline of *lectio divina* is framed by an indispensable set of convictions. The first is that the Bible is the Word of God. It belongs to him. It is from him. It serves his purposes for our lives. The second is that the Spirit who inspired the Scriptures in history speaks through them to us today. The third is that God not only speaks to us through his Word, he seeks to commune with us through his Word. The fourth is that God may speak to us through his Word, and manifest his presence through the Word, in any number of ways, none of which we control. The fifth is that God intends to use all of this to make us more like Christ. We can, and should, cultivate these convictions.

There is a matching set of heart-dispositions that must be present for *lectio divina* to be fruitful in our lives. The first is a hunger and thirst to know God, to know his will, and to know his ways. The second is an unreserved yieldedness to the Spirit who inspired the Word and who dwells within us. The third is an eagerness to hear from God, but a willingness to wait in silence for his voice. The fourth is a radical openness to be addressed by God, to meet with God, in whatever way he chooses. The fifth is a resolve to act on whatever God shows us in ways that will make us more like Christ.

[5] 1 Timothy 4:13. This puts us in a better position to understand Paul's words: "So faith comes from *hearing*, and hearing through the word of Christ." (Romans 10:17)

Reading-as-listening reminds us of the importance of Christian community. While you can and should read and interact with the Scriptures on your own as you cultivate your life with God, it should complement time spent with others in a community of faith. It is good for you to hear others read God's Word, whether it is in the liturgy of a worship service or a group Bible study.

[6] Hebrews 1:1, RSV.

[7] The Bible itself records many ways and instances in which God communicates with his people apart from the Scriptures. Because of who God is in his absolute truthfulness and unwavering trustworthiness, whatever he communicates apart from his written

Word will never contradict or be incompatible with what he has spoken in his written Word. The written Word is the standard against which everything else must be measured. The advantage of listening for the voice of God in *lectio divina* is that it is grounded in and tethered to the written Word.

We should also be very clear that God's communication to us today does not have the status of divine revelation in the Scriptures. The canon is closed. Let none of this, however, deny the reality or diminish the significance of God speaking to his people today. He can and does!

8   Valters Paintner, Wynkoop, *Lectio Divina*, p. 6.

9   Matthew 4:4. We should not miss the fact that Jesus was able to respond to temptation with this Scripture because he likely had meditated on it so often that it came quickly to mind and quickly to his tongue.

10   All Scripture is inspired by God, but not all Scripture has the same purpose. It is a Story, not a collection of timeless axioms. It is the narrative of Redemptive History, which includes many stories of human failure and folly along the way, and much that is background to the Story – the import of which may escape us in our place in history.

To use one of Jesus' metaphors, much of Scripture is like a field in which treasure is buried (Matthew 13:44). Meditation honors the earth that holds the treasure, but seeks the gems that enrich our lives. I don't know, for instance, that the genealogies in the Bible will be fruitful for meditation, but they point to a greater truth that is worthy of our meditation: "When the fullness of time had come, God sent forth his Son, born of woman, born under the law, to redeem those who were under the law." (Galatians 4:3-5)

We have exactly what God wanted us to have in the Bible. We should approach every page with a reverent and thankful heart. In all our reading we should seek the face of God and listen for the voice of God. It is not at all irreverent, however, or errant theology, to recognize that not all Scripture speaks in the same way.

Jesus said that the Scriptures testify to him (John 5:39), and find their fulfillment in him (Luke 24:24-32). If we seek Christ in our meditation, and prayerfully read everything through the lens of the Gospel, the Spirit of God will speak to us through the Word of God.

11   In Latin, *oratio* is a speech. In your *oratio*, you are speaking to God.

12   In Luke 22:42 Jesus prayed, "Father, if you are willing, take this cup from me; yet not my will, but yours be done."

13   1 Samuel 3:9, NIV.

14   See Psalm 141:2.

15   See Romans 8:26-27.

16   *Contemplatio* signifies looking at, gazing at, surveying. This is so, even if it involves ideas and our "mind's eye." According to The Oxford Latin Dictionary, *contemplatio* refers first to "The action of looking at, regarding, view." Its cognate, *contemplo* means "To look at hard, examine visually, gaze at." The *Oxford Latin Dictionary*, ed., P.G.W. Glare (Oxford: Clarendon Press, reprint 1983), pp. 426-27.

17   See, for example, Psalm 25:15; 141:8; Ephesians 1:15-18.

18   Calvin said that in the Scriptures God "lisps with us as nurses are wont to do with little children." John Calvin, *Institutes of the Christian Religion*, trans. Henry Beveridge (Grand Rapids, MI: William B. Eerdmans Publishing Co., eighth printing, 1979), 1.13.1.

19   2 Corinthians 5:13-15

20   2 Corinthians 5:16-17

CHAPTER 7: JOY AND CIRCUMSTANCES: MISUNDER-STANDINGS

1   This line of reasoning fails because it says too little about God. It is not enough to say that God transcends our circumstances. He is also present in them. He is the Ground and Governor of all the circumstances of our lives. A robust understanding of God is essential to our joy.

2   Philippians 4:4

3   I explore this issue in "Joy and the Pursuit of Happiness" in Rick Howe, *Path of Life: Finding the Joy You've Always Longed For* (Boulder, CO: University Ministries Press, 2017).

4   See Philippians 1:18-19.

5   See Philippians 2:19.

6   See Philippians 4:10-11.

7   Quoted in V.J. McGill, *The Idea of Happiness* (New York: Frederick A. Praeger, Publishers, 1967), pp. 15-16.

8   *Pascal's Pensèes,*, trans. W.F. Trotter (New York: E.P. Dutton & Co., Inc., 1958), p. 223.

9   As Aquinas saw it, however, it may well be a foothill on the way to the higher mountain range of joy.

10 Quoted in William G. Morrice, *Joy in the New Testament* (Grand Rapids: William B. Eerdmans Publishing Co., 1984), p. 107.

11 Jesus used this metaphor in Matthew 12:26-29.

12 See, for example, Matthew 5:12; John 15:20; Hebrews 12:8.

13 See Romans 5:3-4.

14 See Hebrews 12:10-11.

15 See James 1:2-4.

16 Prepositions can be theologically significant. After enumerating hardships that believers might endure, including famine, nakedness, danger, and sword, Paul writes (and note the italicized word), "No, *in* all these things we are more than conquerors through him who loved us." See Romans 8:35, 37. We seriously misunderstand God's ways and keep ourselves at arm's length from joy when we don't seek them *in* our circumstances.

17 See John 16:20-22.

18 William Barclay, *The Gospel of Matthew*, Revised Edition (Philadelphia: The Westminster Press, 1975) Vol. I, p. 89.

19 Paul Tournier, *The Adventure of Living*, trans. Edwin Hudson (San Francisco: Harper & Row Publishers, 1965), p. 196.

20 See Hebrews 12:2.

Wilbur Smith wrote:

> When we come to the public ministry of the last days of our Lord we are face to face with a most astonishing fact, namely that it was in the last twenty-four hours of Jesus' life on earth, that He spoke more frequently both of peace and joy than He did in all the rest of His three years of preaching and teaching combined, as far as the records inform us. It was on this last night that Jesus Himself was betrayed by Judas, He was denied by Peter, He was hated by the world, He was rejected by His own brethren, He was mistreated by the soldiers, He was about to suffer every indignity physical and mental. He knew within twenty-four hours He would be nailed to a cross, He was Himself in such agony that He shed as it were drops of blood and cried out that His own soul was exceeding sorrowful even unto death. And yet it was in this very twenty-four hour period, which in many ways may be called the darkest night in human history, that Jesus spoke exclusively of *His own joy*.

Wilbur M. Smith, *Therefore, Stand: Christian Apologetics* (Grand Rapids: Baker Book House, 1945), p. 470.

21 See John 16:33, RSV.

22 William Barclay, *The Letters to the Philippians, Colossians, and Thessalonians*, Revised Edition (Philadelphia: The Westminster Press, 1975) pp. 84-85.

According to Julia Annas,

> The Stoics . . . maintain that the virtuous person is *apathes*, unfeeling, and that virtue requires *apatheia*, absence of feeling or emotion. They stress the importance of the cognitive side of virtue, regarding it in very intellectual ways, and say roundly that there is no degree of feeling that it is appropriate for the virtuous person to have. . . . . the thrust of the thesis is that virtue, far from requiring a settled state of the agent's emotions, demands their elimination.

Julia Annas, *The Morality of Happiness* (New York: Oxford University Press, 1993), pp. 61-62.

23 Matthew 5:4. JB

24 2 Corinthians 6:8-10

CHAPTER 8: FINDING JOY IN THE CIRCUMSTANCES OF LIFE

1 Not to be confused with science, per se. Scientism is a belief-system that includes a commitment to philosophical materialism. It is a quasi-religion in which scientists replace clergy, theories replace doctrines, and evolution replaces creation as a narrative of beginnings. See C.S. Lewis' *The Abolition of Man*, and his space trilogy, *Out of the Silent Planet*, *Perelandra*, and *That Hideous Strength* for his critique of this narrative lie about the world and our place in it. See also Henry F. Schaefer III, "C. S. Lewis: Science and Scientism," found at http://www.lewissociety.org/scientism.php.

2 See Romans 12:2, NIV.

3 It includes, but is more than, a rejection of what is falsely called knowledge. It includes, but is more than, embracing truth-claims grounded in the Scriptures. It includes, but is more than, a "notional understanding" of truth, in the words of Jonathan Edwards. A renewed mind involves a "sense of the heart." See Chapters 5 and 6 for more on this.

4 This could be a good place to pause and review Chapters 5 and 6 on Joy and the Word of God.

[5] Donald G. Bloesch, *Essentials of Evangelical Theology* (San Francisco: Harper & Row Publishers, 1978), Vol. I, p. 30.

[6] Dallas Willard attempts to explore this relationship in *The Divine Conspiracy: Rediscovering Our Hidden Life in God* (San Francisco: Harper San Francisco, 1998), pp. 66ff.

[7] Psalm 119:150-51

[8] "God is our refuge and strength,
   a very present help in trouble." (Psalm 46:1)

(The Psalmist does not say that God is merely present, but *very* present. It is the same adjective used in the creation account when God saw the world that he had made and pronounced it "*very* good." See Genesis 1:31.)

[9] See Psalm 23:4.

[10] See, for example, Psalm 91:4.

[11] See Psalm 139:7-12.

[12] See the classic by Brother Lawrence, *The Practice of the Presence of God.*

[13] See Psalm 16:8.

[14] See Psalm 25:15.

[15] See Psalm 119: 91.

[16] William Shakespeare, *The Complete Works*, ed. Alfred Harbage (Baltimore, Maryland: Penguin Books, 1969), p. 120. Emphasis added.

[17] Romans 8:28. PT

[18] See Acts 17:28.

[19] See Ephesians 1:11-12.

The word rendered "accomplishes" in this verse is the Greek verb *energeo*, from which we get the verb "to energize" and the noun "energy." See also Colossians 1:29 – ""For this I toil, struggling with all his energy that he powerfully works (literally, energizes) within me."

The words *ta panta*, rendered "all things" in Ephesians 1:11 is a typical Pauline way of describing the entire created realm (see, e.g., 1 Corinthians. 8:6; Colossians 1:16-17). God works in, or energizes, the entire creation according to the counsel of his will.

[20] See Colossians 1:16-17 and Hebrews 1:3.

Our word "providence" comes from two Latin words: *pro* (before) and *videre* (to see). To say that God *provides* for us is to say that he sees our needs beforehand (Matthew 6:8) and arranges situations and events to meet them. Divine foreknowledge lies at the heart of this truth.

Put in its simplest terms, God knows everything there is to know. Although it is debated these days, I believe that God's foreknowledge includes future free-willed acts (See next footnote.).

I am sympathetic to the concern of some who think that divine foreknowledge "smothers" human freedom. And it is certainly true that some ways of understanding God's knowledge do that, e.g., the traditional view that God's knowledge is causal: He knows every event in the universe because he causes every event. I think it is better to understand God operating in each sphere according to its nature. While power may be the best way to understand how he works in nature, it is not power, but persuasion, that best fits the *general pattern* of his relationship with rational creatures/moral agents.

Accepting the premise that it is logically possible for God to know future free-willed acts, it seems to me that what God does with his knowledge is still a significant issue. Knowledge can be used to gain an inappropriate advantage over others. It can be used abusively. However, even if one has "inside information" on something, there are still choices to be made about how that knowledge will be used.

We might illustrate a wrongful use of knowledge from "insider trading," when someone in a position to know the finances of a company uses that knowledge in unethical ways in the buying and selling of company stock.

Suppose, however, that a man courting a woman learns from her best friend that she is in a desperate financial situation. He could use that "inside information" to his advantage (if he had the financial resources to do so) to better position himself to win her hand. But what if, instead of giving her money in a way that might make her feel indebted to him – with his knowledge of her situation on the one hand, and his desire to have a relationship in which she loves him for his own sake on the other – he sends money to her anonymously to help her in her time of need? He employs the information in a loving way that respects her and preserves their relationship.

The fact that one has knowledge of a situation, and the use to which that knowledge is put, are two distinct issues. A loving God uses his knowledge in loving ways. A righteous God uses his knowledge in righteous ways. Listen to God's promise in the new covenant: "I will forgive their iniquity, and I will remember their sin no more" (Jeremiah 31:34; see also Hebrews 10:16-17.). This does not mean that God can't remember these things, or that they have literally been removed from the fund of his knowledge. It means that an omniscient God, because he is also merciful, chooses *not* to make use of his knowledge of our sins against us.

It would be consistent with this biblically-based, sound theological principle, to say that while God knows all things (including our future free-willed acts) he chooses to make use of that knowledge in a way that makes room for our freedom, on the one hand, and still preserves his sovereign purposes, on the other. I do not have to know how he actually does this. If it is logically possible, it is sufficient to believe that an omnipotent God could do it.

For a defense of the view that divine foreknowledge is logically compatible with a "libertarian" view of human freedom (as in the next footnote), see, e.g., William Lane Craig, *The Only Wise God: The Compatability of Divine Foreknowledge and Human Freedom*. Grand Rapids, Michigan: Baker, 1987; Stephen T. Davis, *Logic and the Nature of God*. Grand Rapids: Eerdmans, 1983, chapter 4; Alvin Plantinga, *God, Freedom and Evil* (New York: Harper & Row, 1974), pp. 66-72.

[22] In my understanding of freedom, we are free if, given the identical antecedents leading to a decision, we could have chosen otherwise. I would add quickly, however, that though we *could* have done otherwise, in most instances we *would* not have. We only think we would have with the benefit of hindsight. But the addition of a retrospective look at the situation and the events that emerged from it means that the set of antecedents which led to the original decision is no longer intact. The antecedents would no longer be identical. Remove all post-decision factors, replay the exact set of antecedents again, and, even though we could have chosen otherwise, we rarely (if ever?) would.

That we *could* have done otherwise is a metaphysical issue; whether we *would* have done otherwise is a moral issue. It is logically possible that no free moral agent would ever do something differently if presented with exactly the same antecedents. Facing a similar situation, and choosing to respond differently (especially after processing and evaluating our earlier decision and everything that followed from it), is what it means to grow in wisdom. That is another issue.

[23] "Teleological" means directed toward an end, or purposeful.

[24] See Acts 2:23.

[25] Psalm 131:1

[26] While the notion of libertarian freedom (the view described above) best fits the moral reasoning of the Scriptures, "absolute" freedom is a humanistic myth. We are significantly free, but not absolutely free. Our freedom has limits, or boundaries, determined by God.

The book of Job provides us with this insight. Of his work in the realm of nature, God says:

> Or who shut in the sea with doors, when it burst forth from the womb; when I made clouds its garment, and thick darkness its swaddling band, and prescribed bounds for it, and set bars and doors, and said, 'Thus far shall you come, and no farther, and here shall your proud waves be stayed'? (38:10-11, RSV. See also Psalm 104:5-9)

192

The first two chapters of the book of Job show God operating in the same way with moral agents. God gives Satan (an supernatural moral agent, but still a moral agent) freedom to act, but sets the boundaries of his freedom at the same time (1:12; 2:6).

The apostle Paul saw this same pattern to God's relation to human nations: "And he made from one every nation of men to live on all the face of the earth, having determined allotted periods and the boundaries of their habitation" (Acts 17:26, RSV).

When Paul tells believers that God will not allow them to be tested beyond their strength (1 Corinthians 10:13), he is assuring them that God in his sovereign wisdom and loving commitment to them knows where to fix the boundaries in their lives (which includes, in many cases, setting the boundaries of what he will allow other free agents to do to them).

The freedom that God gives always takes place within the boundaries that he has established. They are boundaries of time and place, nature and nurture, and God's own providential acts in the course of life – all of which provide room for a significant degree of freedom, but at the same time protect, preserve and fulfill his sovereign plan.

Although I am wary of some of the ways in which this analogy can be used, there is some merit in seeing similarities between divine providence and a game of chess. God is the Chess Master, and we are on the other side of the board. We have freedom to move our pieces, but it is not absolute. There are limiting factors: the board itself, the chess pieces, the rules of the game, moves that have already been made, moves that will be made by the Master, and our own limitations in the decision-making dynamics of the game. Our freedom has boundaries.

27   As Quoted by Cornelius Plantinga, Jr., *A Place to Stand: A Reformed Study of Creeds and Confessions* (Grand Rapids: The Board of Publications of the Christian Reformed Church, 1979), p. 63.

28   See Ephesians 2:10.

29   See Romans 8:29.

30   2 Corinthians 4:8-9, RSV

31   2 Corinthians 2:14, RSV

32   2 Corinthians 6: 8-10

33   John 16:33, RSV

34   C.S. Lewis says that God brings a complex good from a simple evil:

> In the fallen and partially redeemed universe we may distinguish (1) the simple good descending from God, (2) the simple evil produced by rebellious creatures, and (3) the exploitation of that evil by God for His redemptive

purpose, which produces (4) the complex good to which accepted suffering and repented sin contribute.

C.S. Lewis, *The Problem of Pain* (New York: Macmillan, 1962), p. 111.

35   J.R.R. Tolkien, *The Tolkien Reader* (New York: Ballentine Books, 1966), pp. 86-87.

36   I am indebted to George Eldon Ladd for this insight. See his work, *A Theology of the New Testament* (Grand Rapids: William B. Eerdmans Publishing Co., 1974). To learn more, re-visit Chapter 4 of this book and its exploration of eschatological joy.

37   See Psalm 16:11.

38   C.S. Lewis distinguishes between two kinds of nearness to God: nearness-by-likeness, and the nearness-of-approach. The former is a likeness of natures or attributes between two things. The latter involves progress toward a goal. Lewis writes: If this is what we mean, the states in which a man is "nearest" to God are those in which he is most surely and swiftly approaching his final union with God, vision of God and enjoyment of God. C.S. Lewis, *The Four Loves* (San Diego, New York, London: Harcourt Brace Jovanovich Publishers, 1960), p. 15.

39   Acts 17:28

40   Augustine, "Confessions" in *The Works of Saint Augustine: A Translation for the 21st Century*, ed. John E. Rotelle, trans. Maria Boulding (New York: New City Press, 1997), I/1, p. 83.

41   NIV

42   Psalm 73:23

43   Psalm 73:28

44   See Romans 8:29; 2 Corinthians 3:18.

CHAPTER 9: MARRIAGE: EDEN'S JOY

1   Genesis 1:10, 12, 18, 21, 25, 31

2   Genesis 2:18

3   Karl Barth gave emphasis to this in his understanding of the *imago Dei:*

> "He created them male and female." This is the interpretation immediately given to the sentence "God created man." As in this sense man is the first and

only one to be created in genuine confrontation with God and as a genuine counterpart to his fellows, it is he first and alone who is created "in the image" and "after the likeness" of God.

"And God created man in his image, in the image of God created he him; male and female he created them." . . . Could anything be more obvious than to conclude from this clear indication that the image and likeness of the being created by God signifies existence in confrontation, i.e., in this confrontation, in the juxtaposition and conjunction of man and man which is that of male and female, and then go on to ask against this background in what the original and prototype of the divine existence of the Creator consists? "These two, male and female, are to Him 'man' because they are one before Him. Both are created in this divine image, so that the enjoyment of the divine felicity – to the extent that a creature was made capable of receiving it – was communicated to man as a married couple, filled by God and in God with mutual divine love, from which we may understand and conclude the high dignity of marriage.

Karl Barth, *Church Dogmatics*, eds., G.W. Bromiley, T.F. Torrance (London, New York: T & T Clark International, 2004), Vol. 3.1, pp. 184, 195.

D.S. Bailey writes: "Man . . . is in the image of God in its Manward aspect primarily by virtue of his essential structure as a bi-personal male-female unity in which (relationally . . . not numerically) the coinherence of Father, Son and Holy Spirit is reflected in terms of finite existence." Quoted in Colin Gunton, "The Church on Earth: The Roots of Community," found at: http://theologicaleducationorg.files.wordpress.com/ 2012/03/ gunton.pdf.

[4] Although marriage is an important way in which the image of God is played out in human life, it is not a *necessary property* of the image of God. If it were, the following would necessarily be the case:

> Humans do not bear the image of God outside of marriage (which means, among other things, that children do not).

> Either Jesus failed, or was secretly married as the Gnostics believed.

> Either Jesus was wrong in saying that there would be no marriage in the resurrection, or we will cease to be image-bearers in that state. (Matthew 22:30)

> Both Jesus and Paul were wrong in advocating singleness for the sake of the Kingdom. (Matthew 19:12 and 1 Corinthians 7:8)

There is a better way to understand marriage and the image of God:

> Marriage is not essential, but consequential, to being in the image of God. It is a secondary feature of the image. It adds rich features to our likeness to God.

Gendered relations ("male and female he created them") are fundamental to the image of God regardless of marital status. We are fundamentally made to be beings-in-relation, and this reflects something of the transcendent relations of the persons of the Trinity. Marriage serves the purposes of the *imago Dei* for God's glory and our joy.

5   In Hebrew, man and woman are *ish and ishshah*.

6   Analogy of being (*analogia entis*). It is not a matter of projecting human traits onto our understanding of God. The knowledge *of* God can only be a knowledge *from* God. The analogy is both established and revealed by God.

7   Both the original creation account and Jesus' re-telling of the story to teach about marriage affirm the goodness of sexual intercourse between a man and a woman in a life-long covenant relationship, and do not envision *any* other relationship as an appropriate context for that intimate interaction.

8   A life-long covenant is as close as we come to the eternal bond of love in the Trinity. Divorce diminishes the image of God in the world.

9   Pope John Paul II wrote:

> Man became the 'image and likeness' of God not only through his own humanity, but also through the communion of persons which man and woman form right from the beginning. . . . Right 'from the beginning,' he is not only an image in which the solitude of a person who rules the world is reflected, but also, and essentially, an image of an inscrutable divine communion of persons."

Pope John Paul II, *The Theology of the Body: Human Love in the Divine Plan* (Boston: Pauline Books and Media, 1997), p. 46.

According to Stanley Grenz:

> The meaning of marriage arises out of the place of this institution within the purposes of the Creator. This meaning is enhanced by the biblical use of marriage as a metaphor of God and God's people. However, there remains yet a further dynamic, one which brings together the Old and New Testament uses of the male-female bond. Both in itself and in its relationship to the church, marriage can be a fitting symbol or metaphor of the triune nature of God.

Stanley J. Grenz, *Sexual Ethics: A Biblical Perspective* (Dallas: Word Publishing, 1990), p. 51.

James Torrance has written, "God is love and has his true being in communion, in the mutual indwelling of Father, Son and Holy Spirit . . . This is the God who has created us male and female in his image to find our true humanity in . . . unity with him and one another." James B. Torrance, *Worship, Community and the Triune God of Grace* (Downers Grove: InterVarsity Press, 1996), p. 39.

[10] The Hebrew word translated *help* or *helper*, used of Eve in her relationship with Adam in Genesis 2:18, is *ezer*. I've never understood why some see connotations of inferiority in this title. It seems an odd way of thinking that the one who needs help is superior to the one who provides it. The same word is used of God himself in his relationship with his people. See, for example, Psalm 33:20; 70:5; 115:9; 121:2.

[11] See Genesis 3:20.

[12] The Hebrew word *Adam* was used both of humanity (*mankind*, or *humankind*) as a whole, and of the first man. In the opening chapter of Genesis, *Adam* is the former; in chapter two he is the latter.

[13] I take the verb "to husband," to mean "to steward resources." It comes from an old Norse word which referred to a "tiller of soil." I acknowledge that this meaning is not present in the Hebrew for Adam. It seems fitting, however, for two reasons: 1) In creation, Eve's "man" understood his role in the world to be a steward, including the Garden; 2) In redemption, husbands are charged with stewarding their marriage with the goal of presenting their wives to Christ in the fullness of their feminine glory (Ephesians 5:25-27). I understand this to have a special focus on encouragement and empowerment. Husbands ought to encourage and empower their wives to become all that they can be in Christ.

Stewardship involves the management of something that belongs to someone else. Eve did not belong to Adam, but to God. This truth exposes the lie – wherever it is found – that a wife is the property of her husband. Husbanding and helping both focus on a supportive commitment that enables the beloved to become most fully what God intends him or her to be.

[14] **See** Genesis 2:18.

[15] "Now Adam knew Eve his wife, and she conceived and bore Cain, saying, 'I have gotten a man with the help of the LORD.'" (Genesis 4:1) Because this "knowing," which resulted in the conception and birth of Cain, took place after the expulsion from the Garden, some ancient commentators believed that sex was a result of the Fall. For instance, Augustine wrote, "For it was after they were expelled from it [Paradise] that they came together to beget children, and begot them." Saint Augustine, *The City of God*, trans. Marcus Dods (New York, NY: The Modern Library, 1950), p. 469.

Some believed that the first couple would have had children without sex if they hadn't fallen into sin. John of Damascus (c. 645-749) wrote, "The commandment 'go forth and multiply' does not necessarily mean through conjugal union. For God could increase the human race by another means, if people had preserved the commandment inviolable to the end." Quoted in Vladimir Moss, *Eros in Orthodox Thought*, found at: http://www.romanitas.ru/eng/EROS.htm.

The most that can be said from Genesis 4:1 is that intercourse resulting in pregnancy and childbirth happened after the Fall. Sexual union was clearly envisioned in chapter 1 in the blessing to be fruitful and multiply, and in chapter 2 in the Creator's design for them to be "one flesh" and the fact that they were "naked and unashamed."

If we were to draw any conclusions from Genesis 4:1, it would most naturally be that sex was initially a gift designed solely for the pleasure of Adam and Eve in the "honeymoon" phase of their relationship. When Eve did later conceive, it is as if something new and different had happened in her union with Adam – "with the help of the LORD." Were it not for sin, in time Adam and Eve would have had children in the Garden, and their children would have had children after them. It is not childbearing as such that was introduced in the Curse, but pain in childbearing (Genesis 3:16).

If you embrace the view that human gender and sexuality are part of bearing the image of God, and that sex is as much about the pleasures of an intimate relationship between a husband and wife as it is about procreation, sex before the Fall is exactly what you would expect to have happened. For more on this, see Chapter 13 of this book.

16 Genesis 2:25

17 Singleness and celibacy come into play later in our human story. As Jesus was, we can be fully human and fulfilled in life without marriage. However, that was not God's design for the beginning of our race.

18 For the first couple, their bodies were not the boundaries of their intimacy. More profoundly, it was an entwining of hearts. A giving and receiving of their innermost life. The deep center of their intimacy was a shared worship and a shared joy. A common love for their Creator and mutual pleasure in him. Their love for each other was shaped by their love for him, and kindled by his love for them. Their joy in each other included an awareness of their Maker rejoicing over them, blessing their union, and pleased with their pleasure. Their intimacy was two-fold: husband and wife with each other, and with the God who made them and was present with them in all of life.

19 Genesis 1:28

20 When I give premarital counseling to a couple that does not want or intend to have children, it raises important questions of values that I am compelled to ask: Why would you not want children? Is it possible that what God calls a blessing you see as a burden, or even a curse? If so, that is a problem!

If children are a blessing from the Lord, then couples should at least have what Pope John Paul II called a "procreative attitude," even if they have good reasons for family planning. I agree that this attitude is healthy and important. It means that a husband and wife must "acquire and possess solid convictions about the true values of life and of the family." See Pope John Paul II, *Theology*, p. 399.

21 I understand why one might interpret these words as an imperative. It is grammatically possible. In Hebrew (like the English future tense) the imperfect tense can function to indicate future action or mandated action. Context must help determine which is the

case. When the imperfect tense is used in the language of blessing, it is a forecast of the future enabled and assured by the favor and resources of the one giving the blessing.

22 The Unification Church believes that this, indeed, was Jesus' failure; which is why another Messiah had to come who would fulfill what they take to be a creation mandate.

23 Genesis 1:22

24 See, for example, Deuteronomy 28:1-12.

25 As one scholar puts it: "In the Bible blessing means primarily the active outgoing of the divine goodwill or grace which results in prosperity and happiness amongst men." Alan Richardson, ed., *A Theological Word Book of the Bible* (New York: The Macmillan Co., 1958) p. 33.

26 See Proverbs 18:22.

27 We will see this theme in Song of Solomon for Chapter 12. It is also found in the book of Proverbs. See Proverbs 5:18-19; 30:18-19, RSV.

28 Luther commented:

> For this word which God speaks, 'Be fruitful and multiply,' is not a command. It is more than a command, namely, a divine ordinance which it is not our prerogative to hinder or ignore. Rather, it is just as necessary as the fact that I am a man, and more necessary than sleeping and waking, eating and drinking, and emptying the bowels and bladder. It is a nature and disposition just as innate as the organs involved in it. Therefore, just as God does not command anyone to be a man or a woman but created them the way they have to be, so he does not command them to multiply but creates them so that they have to multiply.

"The Christian in Society" II, in *Luther's Works*, ed. Helmut T. Lehmann (Philadelphia: Muhlenberg Press, 1962), Vol. 45, p. 18.

29 Children are a blessing from God. They are meant for our joy. See Psalm 113:4-9; 127:3, 5; 128:3-4.

30 Some couples are unable to have children as the fruit of their union. On this side of the Garden and the Fall, adoption is a wonderful way of mirroring God's redeeming love for us in Christ!

31 Genesis 3:15, known as the *proto-gospel*:

> I will put enmity between you and the woman,
>   and between your offspring and her offspring;
> he shall bruise your head,
>   and you shall bruise his heel.

Galatians 4:4-5 views this maternal event from the other side: "But when the fullness of time had come, God sent forth his Son, born of woman, born under the law, to redeem those who were under the law, so that we might receive adoption as sons."

The final link in the generational chain involved a Virgin Birth, but this would not have been possible (and the genealogies of Jesus are given to emphasize this) without normal marriage and childbearing for thousands of years leading up to that redemptive event.

[32] In his discussion of the "The Nuptial Meaning of the Body," Pope John Paul II, reflects the Catholic tradition when he speaks of "man's original happiness," and again in his exposition on "The Mystery of Man's Original Innocence." Pope John Paul II, *Theology*, pp. 61 and 67ff.

If I had to guess, Protestant theologians have been reluctant to go there because they want to distance themselves from the Catholic position on original sin and its view of the remnants of the *imago Dei* that have survived the Fall.

[33] This is the joy that Madeleine L'Engle sees captured in the Sanskrit word, *ananda*: "that joy in existence, without which the universe will fall apart and collapse." Madeleine L'Engle, *A Swiftly Tilting Planet* (New York, NY: Dell Publishing, 1979), p. 40. This was not lost entirely in the Fall (Or I would not be here to write this, and you would not be here to read it!), but it was fractured and must be repaired.

CHAPTER 10: MARRIAGE: FAR AS THE CURSE IS FOUND

[1] "For they sow the wind, and they shall reap the whirlwind." (Hosea 8:7)

[2] The heinous moral reality behind "partial birth abortion."

[3] Lyrics by the English hymn writer, Isaac Watts. It was written originally to celebrate the return of Christ at the end of the age, and not his nativity. What will be true in full then can be true now in part.

[4] Restoring the joys of marriage can only happen as those who are married embrace the joys of salvation that we explored in Chapter 4. I can offer no hope and no joy apart from that.

[5] Not all politicians would do this, of course, but those of us who watch the news see such things all too often!

[6] All who sincerely pray, "May your kingdom come, may your will be done on earth as it is in heaven" embrace an ideal that is impossible on human terms. We should not be surprised that this is true when we bring our marriage into that prayer.

[7] See Matthew 19:10.

8   There were two schools of thought on the grounds for divorce. The stricter view was held by Rabbi Shammai, who taught that adultery alone was grounds for divorce. The more liberal view was held by Rabbi Hillel, who taught that a Jewish man could divorce his wife for any reason, from a burnt meal to the discovery of another woman whom he considered more beautiful. The latter was the dominant view in Jesus' day. See, e.g., William Barclay, *The Gospel of Matthew*, revised edition (Philadelphia: The Westminster Press, 1975), Vol. II, pp. 198-199.

9   See Matthew 19:8.

10   Matthew 19:26

11   The first step in reaching any goal is believing that it is possible. For the follower of Jesus this involves believing that something is possible because God himself is involved and invested in the outcome, and then prayerfully acting on that possibility. See the invitation of Jesus in Matthew 17:19-20, Mark 11:22-24, and Luke 17:5-7.

12   Stanley Grenz wrote:

> The concept of trinitarian community is closely related to the divine attribute of love. Throughout the Bible God is presented as the loving one. . . . This assertion suggests that the community that comprises the Godhead is likewise best characterized by reference to the concept of love. The doctrine of the Trinity – the affirmation of one God in three persons – allows this idea to be taken a step further. It indicates that the bonding that characterizes the divine life is similar to the dialectic of sameness and difference found in human sexuality.

Stanley J. Grenz, *Sexual Ethics: A Biblical Perspective* (Dallas, et al.: Word Publishers, 1990), p. 36.

13   I grant that marriage can be viewed as a civil union. Luther saw it that way. This is the realm of government. It is the framework of the contemporary debate about marriage, gender, and sexual orientation. Classically, government would have concerned itself with whether the social order and well-being of citizens is best served by a union between a man and a woman, and by children having both a mother and a father, or by same-gendered partnerships and parenting. In our day the focus has shifted to the pursuit of happiness, however one construes it, and rights to private and public benefits and services.

Whatever you think about these issues, the New Testament sees marriage not as a social contract before human courts, but a sacred covenant before God. There it is portrayed as a relationship between a man and a woman, with Christ as its nexus, summit, and center, and children, if they are granted, as its boon.

It is tragic to see Christians arguing so stridently about civil unions when our own sacred covenants are failing. Nero fiddles while Rome burns! The real power for transforming our culture is not government legislation and the judicial recognition of social contracts (however they are constituted, and however contemporary debates turn out), but the beauty, fragrance, and health of the sacred covenant of marriage on as large a scale as possible.

Even if we have deep moral disagreements over issues of gender identity and sexual orientation, the love we are commanded to show our neighbor includes all without distinction. The command cuts in all directions, and allows no exceptions.

For those who fret about non-traditional civil unions, according to a 2013 national survey reported by the Center for Disease Control and Prevention, only 1.6% of American adults self-identify as gay or lesbian, and only 0.7% consider themselves bi-sexual. Only a fraction of these enter into civil unions. A sense of proportion would be prudent. See http://www.cdc.gov/nchs/data/nhsr/nhsr077.pdf.

[14] See Genesis 1:23-24.

[15] See John 2:1-11 for the story of Jesus' participation in a wedding in Cana, and the performance of his first public miracle.

[16] The chapter in which married women are exhorted to submit to their husbands begins here: "Therefore be imitators of God, as beloved children. And walk in love, as Christ loved us and gave himself up for us, a fragrant offering and sacrifice to God." This is an exhortation to the congregation – men and women alike. (Ephesians 5:1). These words provide the immediate context:

> And do not get drunk with wine, for that is debauchery, but be filled with the Spirit, addressing one another in psalms and hymns and spiritual songs, singing and making melody to the Lord with your heart, giving thanks always and for everything to God the Father in the name of our Lord Jesus Christ, *submitting to one another out of reverence for Christ*. (Ephesians 5:18-21)

In the original Greek, these verses, and the verses that follow, form one long, complex sentence.

[17] Sadly, there are many who use the text in Ephesians 5 to establish a hierarchy in marriage, with husbands lording it over their wives. There is only one Lord, and he did not marry. Mutual submission is nuanced differently for husbands and wives, but it should never be implemented in a way that undoes the mutuality and Christ-centeredness of their humility before each other. Both embrace the heart of *agape*: "My Life For Yours." Thomas Howard, *Hallowed be This House* (San Francisco: Ignatius Press, 1989), p. 47.

In my view, the nuanced mutual submission taught by the apostle Paul is best understood as *preference* and *deference*. A husband is called, in sacrificial love, to give preference to his wife, putting her interests before his own. A wife is called to give loving deference to her husband, putting his interests before her own. It is an expression of mutual honor: "Love one another with brotherly affection. Outdo one another in showing honor." (Romans 12:10) Anything other than this, anything less than this, falls short of what God intends for this relationship.

18 Jonathan Edwards, "The Church's Marriage to Her Sons and to Her God" in *The Works of Jonathan Edwards* (Philadelphia: The Banner of Truth Trust, 1986, Vol. II, pp. 21-22.

19 There is a difference between seeing marriage as sacramental, and regarding it as a sacrament. Protestants (myself included) are willing to affirm the first; Roman Catholics affirm the second. Catholic Christians understand a sacrament not only as a sign and tool of grace, but a conduit of saving grace: God imparts redemptive grace to sinners by virtue of receiving the sacrament. Respectfully, I believe that the Scriptures teach the first but not the second.

20 The English word *mystery* in this text translates the Greek word *mysterion*, which is translated into Latin by the word *sacramentum*. I am not teaching or otherwise affirming the Roman Catholic doctrine that marriage is a sacrament.

CHAPTER 11: MARRIAGE AND FAMILY: EDEN AND MORE

1 1 Corinthians 7:17.

2 Our word "calling" comes from the Greek, *kaleo*. Its Latin equivalent is *vocare*, from which we get the word "vocation.

3 Quoted by Gene Edward Veith at: http://www.modernreformation.org/default.php?page=articledisplay&var1=ArtRead&var2=881.

Gustaf Wingren comments on Luther's view:

> Vocations differ from us: farmers, fishers, and man of all orders, who handle creation's wares, carry God's gifts to their neighbors . . . . God is active in this. There is a direct connection between God's work in creation and his work in these offices. Silver and gold in the earth, growth in the creatures of the forests, the fruitfulness and unquenchable generosity of the soil, all is the ceaseless work of the God of creation, which goes forward through the labors of mankind. God creates the babes in the mother's body – man being only an instrument in God's hand – and then he sustains them with his gifts, brought to the children through the labors of father and mother in their parental office.

Gustaf Wingren, *Luther on Vocation*, trans. Carl C. Rasmussen (Philadelphia: Muhlenburg Press, 1957), p. 9.

4 Quoted in Darby Kathleen Ray, *Working* (Minneapolis: Fortress Press, 2011) p. 74.

5   Robert Kolb and Timothy J. Wenger eds. *The Book of Concord: The Confessions of the Evangelical Lutheran Church*, trans. Charles Arand, et al (Minneapolis: Fortress Press, 2000), pp. 400-401.

6   Paul says that a husband is the "head" of a wife, as Christ is the head of the Church (Ephesians 5:22-24). It seems significant to me that husbands are not addressed in the matter of headship. Wives are. Headship is never something that husbands are told to assert or demand, and never something that gives them permission to insist on their will in marriage. Like respect (Ephesians 5:33), headship is meaningful only if it is a gift freely and lovingly given by a wife, motivated by her reverence for Christ.

In my understanding of a husband's headship in marriage (its sole context), it is not about the rule of a husband over his wife. It is not about authority, but leadership shaped by sacrificial love and a servant's heart – both of which characterized Christ whom they follow. There is a significant difference between a ruler and a leader. Husbands are called to be the latter, but are not authorized by God to be the former. (In the one passage in which husbands and fathers are instructed to "manage" their household, submission is directed to children, not to wives. See 1 Timothy 3:1-5)

For Jesus, a leader serves by leading, and leads by serving. We see this in his characterization of himself as the Good Shepherd (John 10:3-4, 11).

A shepherd leads and lays down his life. Husbands are called to follow Christ in this. Leadership is not about a chain of command, but initiative and influence shaped by a servant's heart. Only this has transformative power for marriages, families, and our world.

7   Inspired by Thomas Howard, *Hallowed be This House* (San Francisco: Ignatius Press, 1989.

8   Paul contrasts this holiness in marriage and family with being "unclean," a ritual term from Jewish law. This may have been in the background of his thought here; however, it would have had no meaning to Gentile believers in Corinth, and no significance for them with respect to Jewish law. Paul means much more by holiness than this.

9   1 Timothy 4:4-5

10   Kolb and Wenger, *The Book of Concord*, p. 414.

11   John Piper, Justin Taylor, eds., *The Supremacy of Sex in Christ* (Wheaton, Illinois: Crossway Books, 2005), p. 235.

12   I am sometimes asked why God does not prevent evil in the world. He doesn't always, to be sure, but I think that he does. What he prevents doesn't happen, and so we are unaware of it. Nevertheless, we have all had uncanny experiences in which we are aware that a potential disaster was averted. An inner voice told us, "Stop!" or moved us in another direction, and we realize that something bad that was about to happen to us did not.

13 Family and government have been designed to restrain evil and promote good in our fallen world. Even with its many flaws, government is better than lawless anarchy. Even in their brokenness and sin, in most cases husbands and wives, and parents and children, are better off living with each other in a marriage and family, than alone and on their own. Even with the problems that can justly be laid at the feet of families and ruling authorities, the world is a much better place than it would be without them. There are glimpses of God's goodness here. His patience. His kindness toward us.

14 In *Path of Life* I wrote:

> But what about the happiness that many seem to experience, when the objects of their desire are good and wholesome, but are pursued and enjoyed without any acknowledgement of God? The desire for marriage is a reflection of God's design. Believers and unbelievers can find happiness there. Parents can find happiness in their children, even if they do not see them as good gifts from God.

Rick Howe, *Path of Life: Finding the Joy You've Always Longed* (Boulder, CO: University Ministries Press, 2017). p. 22.

15 See Malachi 2:16, RSV.

16 See Mark 3:28-30.

17 I know that it may seem implausible and even unthinkable where you are right now, but in some cases a marriage can be restored even after divorce. God receives great glory when grace, mercy, and forgiveness prevail in human hearts, when relationships are restored, and we once again find joy in them.

18 Joy and grace are closely related. The Greek words for grace *charis* (grace) and joy (*chara*) are related to the root, *char*, which centers on the idea of well-being. In classical Greek *charis* (grace) means that which brings well-being, while *chara* (joy) refers the experience of this well-being. See "Grace, Spiritual Gifts" in *The New International Dictionary of New Testament Theology*, ed., Colin Brown (Grand Rapids: Zondervan, 1976) Vol. II, p. 115.

19 Here are the relevant passages in the New Testament on this: Matthew 19:1-9; Mark 10:1-12; 1 Corinthians 7:10-16.

20 See Hebrews 13:4.

21 Behind the word "repentance" in the New Testament is the Greek word "metanoia" – a change of mind, heart, or purpose. Repentance is a change of mind that results in a change of direction and a change of life. It is rejecting the views of a sinful world, embracing God's perspective, and aligning your life with what God says.

22 See Psalm 51:12.

23   I recognize that in some cases a sexual relationship in marriage is not physically possible, or may not be as robust as might be otherwise desirable. This is especially true as age advances. Apart from these conditions, however, unless for temporary respites for the spiritual disciplines of prayer, celibacy within marriage is dysfunctional. There are unhealthy conditions involved, whether they are personal (stress, anxiety), relational (unresolved anger, self-centeredness, etc.) or theological (the error that in God's eyes abstinence is better than enjoying the pleasures of this gift). God does not call people to marriage and to celibacy at the same time!

24   1 Corinthians 7:6-7

25   Which is why Jesus taught that all who follow him must be prepared to lose these important relationships for his sake.

CHAPTER 12: MARRIAGE AND FAMILY: LOVE'S DELIGHTS, PART 1

1   In this chapter and the next I will explore the loves *storge*, *philia*, *eros*, and *agape*. In his classic work, *The Four Loves*, C.S. Lewis charted the course for this, examining our experience of love through the lens of each of these loves. See C.S. Lewis, *The Four Loves* (San Diego, New York, London: Harcourt Brace Jovanovich Publishers, 1960).

2   "Anyone who does not love does not know God, because God is love." (1 John 4:8)

3   Josef Pieper, *About Love* (Chicago: Franciscan Herald Press, 1974), p. 71.

4   David W. Gill, *Becoming Good: Building Moral Character* (Downers Grove, Illinois: InterVarsity Press, 2000), p. 54.

5   C.S. Lewis, *The Four Loves*, p. 53. While this word is not used by writers of the New Testament, the love to which it points is described in other ways throughout the Scriptures.

6   Conversely, *storge* can exist without *philia*, *eros* and *agape*, but it is greatly impoverished without them. Many marriages endure on the basis of *storge* alone. Husbands and wives become comfortable living together and playing their respective familial roles. Often they have spent their love energy on their children, and have never developed the other dimensions of love. They stay together for the children, and may or may not stay together when their nest is empty. If they do, it is only because they prefer the status quo of *storge* to the alternatives. As important as this humble love is, there is so much more in God's design for marriages and families. There is much more joy to be gained!

7   C.S. Lewis, *The Four Loves*, p. 20.

8   The appropriate heart-response is thanksgiving, and treasuring his gifts with loving care. Without this love, neglect on the one hand, or abuse on the other, destroys the joy that God intends for us in these relationships. It is the waning of this love in our culture that has made the abortion industry possible. Whatever else may be the case when the life of a little one is ended, love has grown cold. Jesus said that this would be true: "And because lawlessness will be increased, the love of many will grow cold." (Matthew 24:12)

9   C.S. Lewis, *The Four Loves*, p. 54.

10   Jesus introduced his followers to God as *Abba*, the intimate, endearing name of a child for her daddy. He provides, protects, and loves us with or without our merit, simply because he is our Father and we are his children. See, for example, Matthew 6:7-13; 6:31-32; Luke 11:11-13)

God's parental love for us is portrayed with maternal images, as well, including pictures of a mother bird and even a mother bear. See, for example, Deuteronomy 32:10-12; Ruth 2:12; Psalm 17:8; 57:1; Hosea 13:4-8; Matthew 23:37. God is also pictured as a human mother: Isaiah 42:1; 49:15; 66:13.

11   Jesus' story is told in Luke 15:11-32.

12   See Exodus 20:12.

13   Robert Kolb and Timothy J. Wenger eds. *The Book of Concord: The Confessions of the Evangelical Lutheran Church*, trans. Charles Arand, et al (Minneapolis: Fortress Press, 2000), p. 401.

14   Luke 2:52

15   Martin Luther, "The Christian in Society" II, in *Luther's Works*, ed. Helmut T. Lehmann (Philadelphia: Muhlenberg Press, 1962), Vol. 45, p. 46.

16   Luther, "Sermons," *Luther's Works*, Vol. 51, p. 363.

17   Jonathan Edwards saw the Christian family as a "little church."

> Every Christian family ought to be as it were a little church, consecrated to Christ, and wholly influenced and governed by his rules. And family education and order are some of the chief of the means of grace. If these fail, all the means of grace are like to prove ineffectual. If these are duly maintained, all the means of grace will be like to prosper and be successful.

Jonathan Edwards, *A Farewell Sermon* (Minneapolis, MN: Curiosmith, 2011), p. 56.

18   If you can't live near family, you can still prioritize family love with reunions, holidays, and family vacations. Thankfully, in a day when families often live apart from each other, we have technologies that make digital real-time audio-visual interaction possible.

19 C.S. Lewis, *The Four Loves*, p. 88.

20 Ibid., pp. 98-99.

21 The elimination of boys and girls clubs and athletic teams and gender-specific groups for men and women in the interests of "gender equality" betray either profound ignorance or monumental folly.

22 Song of Solomon 5:16

23 Friendship can exist between spouses when their shared interest is their children. If this is the only basis for friendship, however, their relationship can be jeopardized when their children become adults with interests, concerns and commitments of their own.

24 This doesn't mean that Christians can only befriend fellow Christians. Friendships can be based upon creation values and common pleasures with those who may not yet share an interest in Christ.

25 See, for example, Jesus' words to his followers in John 15:13,14 and 15.

26 C.S. Lewis, *The Last Battle* (New York: Collier Books, 11th printing, 1974), p. 154.

Chapter 13: Marriage and Family: Love's Delights Part 2

1 C.S. Lewis, *The Four Loves* (San Diego, New York, London: Harcourt Brace Jovanovich Publishers, 1960), p. 131. Like *storge*, this word is not used by New Testament writers, probably, in this case, because it was too closely associated with views of sexuality that were utterly incompatible with a Christian vision of life. I include it because it helps us elucidate a biblical vision of romantic and sexual love.

2 I have had many occasions over the years to give counsel to young men during their university years who struggle with lust. My advice for them (which would be the same for women) encourages four movements of the heart: confession, affirmation, denial, embrace.

First, we all stumble and fall in many ways, and lust trips us up as often as anything. Let lust drive you to your knees before God's throne of grace. In that place of humility, confess your sins of lust, your need for his mercy and your complete dependence upon his gracious help. That is a healthy place for sinners to be!

Second, with thanksgiving, affirm the goodness of God's world, and the goodness of his workmanship in you, including your sexuality. Thank him for feminine beauty! If you are a woman struggling with this, thank him for masculine attractiveness! If you are married, thank God for your wife or your husband. If you hope to be married but

208

aren't yet, thank him for the husband or wife he is preparing for you. Affirm the goodness of marriage and family in God's wise design for life.

Third, deny yourself. Sexual pleasure in God's design is always a gift to be given, not a prize to be taken. It is to be given and received *only* in marriage. Whether you are married or single, say "no" to any desire for "conquest," or "having" or "having your way" with someone. Whether you are married or single, say "no" to sex outside of marriage. Saying "no" to yourself also means saying "no" to putting yourself in situations in which you are exposed to lust's temptations. The apostle Paul told his young friend, Timothy, to "flee useful lusts." That includes the Internet, television, movies, books, magazines, and any settings of immodesty or impropriety. This is getting harder and harder to do in our world, but it is still essential to following Christ.

Fourth, embrace the fullness of life that God wants for you, that Christ came to secure for you, and that the Holy Spirit will empower you to have. It is the life of joy that I have tried to describe in *Path of Life* and *River of Delights*. The more you pursue joy, the less power lust will have over you (since the pleasures of lust are a cheap substitute for joy, and are only attractive to those who do not know joy and its ways).

If you are single, there is more helpful information for you at the end of Chapter 11.

[3] C.S. Lewis, *The Four Loves*, pp. 134-135.

[4] Pope John Paul II saw lust for one's spouse as impossible by the nature of the case. "This lustful look, if addressed to his own wife, is not adultery 'in his heart.' This is precisely because the man's interior act refers to the woman who is his wife, with regard to whom adultery cannot take place." Pope John Paul II, *The Theology of the Body: Human Love in the Divine Plan* (Boston: Pauline Books and Media, 1997), p. 107.

I agree that lust is a sin against marriage. There is a relational sin involved in looking at someone other than your spouse, and fantasizing sexual relations with him or her. That pleasure is prohibited by the Creator outside of marriage. Lust is not only a sin against the institution of marriage, however, it is a sin against your spouse if you are married, and a sin against your future spouse if you are not yet married.

This is lust, but lust is more than this. There is more than one problem with this sin.

Lust is a sin against our own bodies (in the same way that uniting with a prostitute is, according to the apostle Paul in 1 Corinthians 6:15-18). The desire for sexual pleasure in itself is good. God has made us sexual beings. In our fallen world, however, apart from God's grace to us in Christ, the desire for sexual pleasure becomes distorted, warped and twisted. We sin against our own sexuality when we seek gratification outside the context of marriage.

Further, lust is a sin against the Holy Spirit, whose presence within us makes our bodies a temple. We are called to glorify God in these temples, but sexual immorality, including lust, dishonors our divine Guest (1 Corinthians 6:18-20).

Lust is a sin against the image of God in another person: a sin against another human being by objectifying him or her, and treating him or her as a means to sexual gratification – even if it is done in the heart and not by physical touch. The victims of lust cease to be regarded as persons made in the image of God, and are reduced to sex objects. Sources of sexual stimulation. Lust is concerned with "having" or "having one's way" with another person. Lust regards another person as an object; Love regards the other as a rightful Subject. Love expresses itself within the context of an I-Thou relationship. Lust reduces the relationship to I-it. Sadly, this sinful dimension of lust can be found both within and outside of marriage.

Finally, lust is a sin against joy. It was the observation of another Roman Catholic, Thomas Aquinas, that the person who is "deprived of spiritual joy goes over to carnal pleasures." Lust is declining God's intended gift of joy, going over to his adversary's side, and plundering another person for self-gratification. It also ignores the deeper, spiritual, and sinful nature of lust as a substitute for joy. God intends something far better for us! He desires greater and greater experiences of his joy – which embraces all the healthy pleasures in life, including sex within marriage.

5 J.I. Packer summarizes patristic thought on sexual relations in marriage:

> Chrysostom had denied that Adam and Eve could have had sexual relations before the Fall; Augustine allowed that procreation was lawful, but insisted that that the passions accompanying intercourse were always sinful; Origen had inclined to the theory that had sin not entered the world the human race would have been propagated in an angelic manner, whatever that might be, rather than by sexual union; and Gregory of Nyssa was sure that Adam and Eve had been made without sexual desire, and that had there been no Fall mankind would have reproduced by means of what Leland Ryken gravely calls "some harmless mode of vegetation." The Fathers' background was the decadent Graeco-Roman culture that had systematically debased marriage and sexual relations for centuries, so perhaps, they, too, should not be blamed too much for views such as these. It is obvious, however, that so twisted a record needed to be set straight, and this the Reformers, followed by the Puritans, forthrightly did.

J.I. Packer, *A Quest for Godliness: The Puritan Vision of the Christian Life* (Wheaton, IL: Crossway Books, 1990), p. 261.

6 *The Library of Christian Classics, Volume II, Alexandrian Christianity*, trans. John Ernest Leonard Oulton and Henry Chadwick (Philadelphia: The Westminster Press, 1954), p. 67.

7 Jerome, "Against Jovinianus," 1:49, available online at:
http://www.ccel.org/ccel/schaff/npnf206.vi.vi.I.html.

8 Augustine, "Marriage and Virginity" in *The Works of Saint Augustine: A Translation for the 21ˢᵗ Century*, ed. John E. Rotelle, trans. Ray Kearney (New York: New City Press, 1999), I/9, p. 35.

Augustine wrote:

> What friend of wisdom and holy joys, who being married . . . would not prefer, if this were possible, to beget children without this lust, so that in this function of begetting offspring by the members created for this purpose should not be stimulated by the heat of lust, but should be actuated by his volition, in the same way as his other members serve him for their respective ends?

> [In Paradise before the Fall] The man, then, would have sown the seed, and the woman received it, as need required, the generative organs being moved by the will, not excited by lust.

> In such happy circumstances and general well-being we should be far from suspecting that offspring could not have been begotten without the disease of lust, but those parts, like all the rest, would be set in motion at the command of the will; and without the seductive stimulus of passion, with calmness of mind and with no corrupting integrity of the body, the husband would lie upon the bosom of his wife.

Saint Augustine, *The City of God*, trans. Marcus Dods (New York, NY: The Modern Library, 1950), pp. 464-75. In his interpretation of Genesis, he wrote:

> Why, therefore, may we not assume that the first couple before they sinned could have given a command to their genital organs for the purpose of procreation as they did to other members which the soul is accustomed to move to perform various tasks without any trouble and without any craving for pleasure? For the almighty Creator, worthy of praise beyond all words, who is great even in the least of His works, has given to the bees the power of reproducing their young just as they produce wax and honey.

Augustine, *The Literal Meaning of Genesis*, trans. John Hammond Taylor, in *Ancient Christian Writers: The Works of the Fathers in Translation* (New York, NY/Ramsey, NJ: 1982), No. 42, Vol. II, p. 81.

[9] Quoted in Vladimir Moss, *Eros in Orthodox Thought*, found at: http://www.romanitas.ru/eng/EROS.htm.

[10] Quoted in John Witte, Robert McCune Kingdon, *Sex, Marriage, and Family in John Calvin's Geneva: Courtship, Engagement and Marriage* (Grand Rapids: Wm. B. Eerdmans Publishing Co., 2005), p. 282.

See also *John Calvin's Sermons on the Ten Commandments*, ed. and trans. Benjamin W. Farley (Grand Rapids, MI: Baker Book House, 1980), p. 180: "When men and women keep themselves within the bounds of the fear of God and complete modesty, the [marriage] bed is honorable. . . . What the apostle calls honorable in God's sight is hardly a mere trifle. . . ."

11   Quoted in Timothy J. Wengert, *Harvesting Martin Luther's Reflections on Theology, Ethics, and the Church* (Grand Rapids, MI: Wm. B. Eerdmans Publishing Co., 2004), p. 184.

12   Thomas Hooker, Puritan leader and founder of the colony of Connecticut, wrote of this affection: "The man whose heart is endeared to the woman he loves, he dreams of her in the night, hath her in his eye and apprehension when he awakes, museth on her as he sits at table, walks with her when he travels and parlies with her in each place where he comes." Quoted in J.I. Packer, *A Quest for Godliness*, p. 265.

Augustine made this distinction between desire and joy: "When consent takes the form of seeking to possess the things we wish, this is called desire; and when consent takes the form of enjoying the things we wish, this is called joy." And, "The right will is, therefore, well-directed love, and the wrong will is ill-directed love. Love then, yearning to have what is loved, is desire; and having and enjoying it, is joy." *Augustine, City of God*, pp. 448-49.

13   Josef Pieper, *About Love,* trans., Richard and Clara Winston (Chicago: Franciscan Herald Press, 1974), p. 74.

14   John MacQuarrie writes, "As a relationship develops there is less awareness of giving and receiving as separate acts – gradually the giving and receiving are recognized only as part of the single act of sharing." From the article, "Blessedness" in *The Dictionary of Christian Ethics* (Philadelphia: The Westminster Press, 1967), p. 33.

15   Lewis uses this word for love more narrowly than it is used in classical Greek, or even in the *Septuagint*, the ancient Greek translation of the Hebrew Scriptures, where it often overlaps with other Greek words for love. His use is shaped by classical texts in the New Testament, and then shaped by Christian tradition. This is the way that I am using the word.

16   Thomas Howard, *Hallowed be This House* (San Francisco: Ignatius Press, 1989), pp. 46-47.

17   C.S. Lewis, *The Four Loves*, p. 166.

18   "Anyone who does not love does not know God, because God is love." (1 John 4:8)

19   See James 1:17.

20   Acts 17:25

21   See John 3:16

22   See Mark 10:45.

23   See John 7:39; Acts 5:32; Romans 5:5.

24   See 1 Corinthians 2:12; 1 Corinthians 12:7; 2 Corinthians 1:22; 5:5.

212

25   C.S. Lewis, *The Four Loves*, p. 169.

26   The little prophetic book of Hosea tells the story of this sorrow. Like Hosea, the Lord is a faithful, loving husband to his people; like Gomer, the prostitute-wife, Israel spurned the love of God.

27   Universalism, the view that in the end God's love will triumph and that all will be reconciled with God, is as old as Origen (c. 185-254) and as recent as Rob Bell, *Love Wins: A Book About Heaven, Hell, and the Fate of Every Person Who Ever Lived* (New York: HarperCollins, 2011). In my view this not only fails to square with the teaching of Jesus and the apostles, it misunderstands divine love and human freedom in God's redemptive plan. God allows us to say "No" to his love. If that is so, and we turn out to be immortal after all, there must be a place for those who make that choice. That is hell.

28   In the place of God. Jesus is not merely speaking of his trips to Jerusalem and the times that he had grieved its spiritual condition. This is the voice of God expressing the heart of God over the centuries.

29   Matthew 23:37

30   C.S. Lewis describes the costliness of this love:

> God, who needs nothing, loves into existence wholly superfluous creatures in order that He may love and perfect them. He creates the universe, already foreseeing . . . the buzzing cloud of flies about the cross, the flayed back pressed against the uneven stake, the nails driven through the mesial nerves, the repeated incipient suffocation as the body droops, the repeated torture of back and arms as it is time after time, for breath's sake, hitched up.

C.S. Lewis, *The Four Loves*, p. 176.

31   Romans 5:6-8

32   See 1 Peter 3:18.

33   See Galatians 5:22-23.

34   John 15:13, NIV. The Greek word for "love" used in this verse is *agape*; the word for "friends" is *philos*.

35   Song of Solomon 6:3

36   C.S. Lewis, *The Four Loves*, p. 177.

37   James E. Gilman, *Fidelity of Heart: An Ethic of Christian Virtue* (Oxford: Oxford University Press, 2001), p. 54.

38   Thomas Howard, *Hallowed be This House*, pp. 13-14.

Made in the USA
Monee, IL
03 January 2021

56149286R00125